The Least You Should Know about Therapy

The Least You Should Know about Therapy

By: Dr. Kimberly L. Olson, Ph.D., LMFT

The Least You Should Know about Therapy

Copyright © 2023 Dr. Kimberly L. Olson, Ph.D., LMFT

Author: Dr. Kimberly L. Olson, Ph.D., LMFT

Cover Design: Darío de los Santos

ISBN 979-8-9875674-0-1

$19.99

ISBN 979-8-9875674-0-1

51999>

9 798987 567401

*Dedicated to a **Loving God**
who has always worked through people in my life.
May I be a demonstration of you love and character always.*

Special Thanks:

*To my parents and sister, who loved me enough to ensure
that I got the help I needed and were humble enough to
recognize that recovery involved the whole family. Thank you
for taking the journey with me, even when it cost you a lot.*

*To Gail Posner, LCSW, the therapist who nurtured and
advocated for a broken child, and inspired her to become a
therapist.*

*To Vivian Klauber, Ruty Bladderman (Rest in Peace), Carl
Thiele, and all of the staff and clients of the defunct Abbott
Northwestern Willow Street Center.*

*To Alexandra James who brought purpose and meaning to
my life.*

*To Dr. Edward & Faith Teyber (Rest in Peace), who taught
me the true meaning of being a therapist and inspired me to
teach others.*

*To David Olson, Betty Murphy, and Sandra Chavez,
my corrective emotional experiences.*

*To all of my family, friends, mentors, and colleagues,
for your inspiration, love, and support!*

*To all of my clients for sharing your journey and recovery
with me. I am humbled and honored by your strength and
trust. I pray to be worthy of your confidence and forgiven
when I fall short.*

"Nobody cares how much you know,
until they know how much you care."

-Theodore Roosevelt

Preface

Over the past 20 years, the quality of psychotherapy has decreased with tales of empathic failure running rampant. The clients are suffering, as is the credibility of the profession. With more emphasis on evidence-based practices than ever, it seems inconsistent that the quality of care would decrease.

While reviewing the literature and examining client complaints, it has become evident that many training programs no longer emphasize the therapeutic relationship, which is the greatest predictor of outcomes. While a variety of reasons exist for this lack of training, the impact is being experienced by the clients who report feeling invalidated and consequently, terminate prematurely. The therapist may or may not understand what has occurred to elicit this response.

The book aims to introduce the essential components of the therapeutic relationship in a simple, accessible way. Exercises and worksheets will make the information meaningful and applicable to the reader. The introduction of the Relational Chart® format creates a structure for otherwise ambiguous concepts, and makes the relationship among variables evident. The author intends to familiarize new therapists with the therapeutic relationship to improve the quality of care for the clients and the efficacy of new therapists.

Contents

Chapter 1: Introduction

The Problem

The client is a 55-year-old Caucasian female who requested therapy for depression from a telehealth program. The client was asked to complete a brief questionnaire before intake and indicated that she has an extensive history of therapy, but hasn't attended in 20 years. The client noted that she's currently experiencing a severe depressive episode and suicidal ideation (no plan or intent). The questionnaire also included demographic information, and the client indicated that she is married, has two adult children and has been a School Counselor for over 20 years.

A therapist contacted the client, and they agreed to meet via telehealth. They could not get connected (due to a problem with the link), so they rescheduled for the following week. Feeling even more desperate and concerned about connecting this week, the client emailed the therapist asking, "If for whatever reason, we cannot connect this time, may we speak by phone? I really need to talk to someone." The therapist responded, "We will be meeting by telehealth only." Feeling invalidated and frustrated, the client requested another provider willing to meet by phone.

The second therapist contacted the client by email and requested that the client complete a "Goal Setting" worksheet (something the client used to assist high school students in career planning) before their first meeting. The client thought, "You can't be serious! We haven't even met. Do you think a school counselor needs a lesson on goal setting?" Nevertheless, based on the client's background as a school counselor, she responded to the email with the following: "Let's discuss this, as well as our mutual expectations of therapy during our first session." This discussion never occurred.

The first session went fairly well, despite different expectations of therapy. The therapist validated the client's emotions, and while never agreeing to use a thought record, the client found it beneficial, noting a core belief, "I am alone." The client thought, "It's good to have a different perspective, and I suspect I will learn a lot." The client was very enthusiastic.

The truth is that by the time the client spoke with the second therapist, she was so desperate to be heard, that she was willing to overlook any potential problems. It had been a pattern in the client's life to "accept whatever scraps" she was lucky enough to receive and to worship the provider of said scraps. The client experienced ambivalence to the extent that she believed she was too needy and expecting too much, but also felt angry over not even being asked for her input by the therapist.

The second session went predictably wrong. The therapist had forgotten the thought record and the important core belief, which made the client feel invalidated and think, "I'm not even important to the guy I'm paying to care for me." The client didn't say anything, as she too understood what it was like to keep many students' stories straight, but more importantly, it would have been shameful to admit such vulnerability. The client redirected the emotions of this exchange to a significant issue of abuse that was deeply emotional and troubling. The therapist instructed the client to get a piece of paper, because "We're going to do the WISEMIND (as cited in Tanning, 2019) exercise to teach you emotional regulation." The client was beside herself. The client tearfully said, "This isn't going to work for me, and I need to end the call for today. I teach this too, but it's not what I need right now." The therapist said, "Okay," and ended the session. Five minutes later, the therapist sent the client an email stating that the telehealth site had other therapists to choose from. The client hasn't been back to that site or any other therapist. *Why?*

The American Psychological Association (2022, APA Dictionary) defines empathic failure as "a lack of understanding of another person's feelings, perception and thoughts." O'Rear (2014) adds, "Our emotional reactions or misjudgments as therapists result in us having a huge lapse in empathy and completely missing our clients." It is strongly suspected that neither therapist acted with malice or forethought, but reenacted damaging themes for the client, instead of providing a corrective emotional experience (Miller, 2021). As the client shared these experiences with the author, she was struck by how frequently (especially in the past 15 years) she's heard this narrative.

There were numerous examples of empathic failure in the vignette above. The client felt unimportant to the first therapist, as her pleas for an alternate contact method fell upon deaf ears. The second therapist failed to consider how a goal-setting activity might be received from a well-educated, school counselor, or any client. The therapist did not follow-up regarding the client's request to discuss expectations of therapy, which would have clarified this and minimized disappointed expectations. The therapist didn't review progress notes regarding the previous session (which had been powerful for the client), so what felt like a provisional bond was invalidated. The therapist did not respond to the client's distress, but instead attempted to implement an intervention that wasn't appropriate or well-received in this case. The therapist did not respond to prompting to explore why the client ended the session early or provide an empathic response to the client's distress. Finally, the therapist provided referrals rather than reaching out to the client, which suggested termination and abandonment.

The therapists' perspectives were likely quite different. The first therapist perhaps felt that the client was attempting to receive special treatment, and the therapist was setting a boundary. It could be that the first therapist wouldn't get paid if the session occurred outside of the network, so the therapist's reasonable concerns about payment may have usurped the client's welfare. The second therapist may have thought that the client wouldn't dictate therapy, when he was the expert. The client ending the session early may have been perceived as manipulation. The second therapist's insistence on certain activities may reflect anxiety over a lack of diversified training, discomfort with emotions, and/or an inability to respond.

It likely never occurred to either therapist that they were dealing with a truly desperate, suicidal person. Due to pride, shame, and fear that her needs would not be met, the client delayed help seeking as long as possible. Months building up to seeking treatment had been riddled with tears, suicidal ideation, and desperation, although she kept this contained around others. When the client and first therapist experienced technical difficulties, the client was gracious towards the therapist, but privately cried and thought, "I can't even get help when I pay for it."

The client had not intended to terminate with the second therapist, but to regroup and find a way to communicate her needs, while honoring his. The therapist terminated therapy, or abandoned the client, which left the client feeling once again that her needs were too much and reinforced the core belief, "I am alone." What if the client had committed suicide following these exchanges? Would the therapist be liable for malpractice? Probably not legally, but what about ethically? Morally?

Empathic failure is the most commonly cited reason for premature termination (Ardito & Rabellino, 2011; O'Rear, 2014). Being a Clinic Supervisor for 12 years, I have read well over 200 "Change of Provider" request forms. The majority of clients requesting a change of provider reported some version of feeling judged, invalidated, and/or dismissed by the provider. Like the example of the school counselor, often the therapist's reaction to the client mirrors the client's experiences with others, which may be due to eliciting maneuvers (Teyber, 2000). While therapists are not mind readers, we should be trained to explore the dynamics that could predict empathic failure or the corrective emotional experience. It's unclear that this training is being done today.

Introduction

My name is Kimberly Olson, and I am a Licensed Psychologist and Marriage and Family Therapist who has been practicing therapy for over 20 years, as well as supervising and teaching therapy students and interns (associates). For the past 12 years, I've been a Clinic Supervisor for county mental health. We often have staff only long enough for the intern (associate) to become licensed and move onto a less stressful and significantly better-paying job. My reality is that I'm training new therapists constantly, which gives me some insight into our current university and training programs and what appears to be missing.

There has been an educational shift in therapy training programs. My early interns demonstrated a baseline knowledge of the dynamics of the therapeutic relationship, which made training much easier. In the last decade (or more) however, interns are coming to the clinic with little or no training on the therapeutic relationship, which is a significant determining factor of therapeutic outcomes (Ardito & Rabellino, 2011; DeAngelis, 2019; Stargell, 2017). Most interns have a grasp of several evidence-based practices, which is terrific, but lack the knowledge of why a client will or will not be receptive to them or their practices.

There appears to be several misconceptions about the therapeutic relationship. Interns seem to understand the Rogerian triad (empathy, congruence, and unconditional positive regard), but that seems to be the alpha and omega of their training (Ardito and Rabellino, 2011). An intern once told me, "I'm a very kind and sensitive person, believe me, so I don't need relationship training." The intern (in fact) was a very kind and sensitive person, but completely clueless about the therapeutic relationship.

I like to start my classroom lectures about the therapeutic relationship with the following question: "What's the difference between counseling and therapy?" If your response is "nothing" or "very little," I'm especially glad you're reading this book. Therapist training has become so marginalized that many therapists don't even know the difference.

Counseling is generally short-term, problem-solution focused, advice giving, and; the counselor is the expert. Counseling is extremely valuable, as potentially life-threatening issues like domestic violence and substance dependency require a directive, immediate approach. Additionally, clients can gain many empowering skills from counseling, and our society loves instant gratification and counseling! Oprah, Dr. Phil, and the University of YouTube have created an intellectual, skill-based culture that has benefitted society in innumerable ways. However, it has also left society (and some therapists) unable to distinguish therapy from other forms of self-help. *Unfortunately, the lack of training in relational dynamics in many current therapy programs has contributed to our devaluation and without rectification, our demise.*

Therapy is person-centered, as opposed to problem-centered. It's where you go after counseling has failed. It's where you go when your incredible knowledge continues to fail to yield *long-term results*. It's where you go when you know WHAT to do (maybe even better than your therapist), but you fail to do it. In a word, it's where you go when you're "stuck". If you could change and get "unstuck" with counseling, you wouldn't likely need therapy. Therapy is concerned with identifying patterns (themes) of relationships, moods, cognitions, behaviors, pathogenic beliefs and core beliefs that occur across situations and generally throughout the lifespan. It's your *automatic pilot*, or what you revert to after each failed attempt at change. Therapy is concerned with finding a skeleton key that will not just solve a problem, but change a lifetime of destructive behaviors and interactions; thus, changing the person.

Based on this definition, it should be evident that therapy will rarely be a six-sessions or less proposition. Have you ever trusted someone after knowing them for only six hours? Me either. It also requires depth and insight, something that not all therapists (or people) have, especially now that the selection process (in some cases) for therapy training programs has all but been narrowed to the capacity to obtain a student loan. Historically, student therapists had to compete for program admission, which required competitive grades, participation in research and publication, community internships, complex interviews, etc. While this didn't guarantee a quality therapist, it suggested a baseline of intelligence (a prerequisite for insight), capability, and a deep dedication to learning and to the profession. These full-time programs required most of the students' time and attention. Today, it's not uncommon for students to obtain a master's degree as an adjunct to full-time employment, family… and everything else. Education may be the student's second or third priority with minimal effort (relatively speaking) being exercised to obtain a master's degree. It is no wonder that the more complex skills are not being taught, and the quality of therapy has suffered.

The former competitive selection process, however, also had a significant downfall to the extent that many insightful people with real-world experience would be excluded from the selection process. People living in an ivory tower are not always the most relatable to desperate people. Many of my students in non-traditional programs are extremely insightful, as they have an internal frame of reference that often generates prompt and accurate working hypotheses. These students also tend to be very likable, which isn't the purpose of therapy, but it's certainly beneficial in relationship building.

As long as education is financially motivated, there will not be a return to rigid standards, but the absence of understanding of the therapeutic relationship can't continue either. Clients are getting hurt (Ardito & Rabellino, 2011). Many would-be therapists don't even understand what is unique about our profession and consequently, why *not everyone can do it*. At this point, a veteran therapist may ask, "Are you proposing that we return to a long-term psychodynamic approach? I will be out of business!" No, although I don't think it's a coincidence that empirical support for short-term models, and the vilification of more dynamic models seemed to rise with the prevalence of Health Maintenance Organizations (HMO) (Hutchings, 2022). I am suggesting is that we utilize the priceless concepts from these camps that contribute to the therapeutic relationship, ultimately making clients more receptive to therapy, regardless of orientation.

Chapter 2: What is the Therapeutic Relationship?

S imply stated, it's the relationship between you and your client ... and every relationship the client has experienced before you. It's transference (e.g., reacting to the therapist based on the client's previous experiences and assumptions); it's countertransference (e.g., the therapist's reaction to the client's transference and/or reacting based on the therapist's personal experiences). Transference can be positive or negative. Most relationships however are a combination of positive and negative traits, but understanding Bowlby's (1958) Internal Working Model is fundamental to forming and maintaining a therapeutic relationship (as cited in Li, 2022).

For example, I noticed that a female client (Sarah) had lost a lot of weight. I knew that she had been dieting and working hard for this change. I said, "Wow! You can tell that you've lost weight. I can especially see it in your face." The client paused, glared and responded, "Just in my face, huh? You're saying the rest of my body looks terrible?!" I could have responded with complete empathic failure, if I didn't understand the client's internal working model. Instead, I made the following process comment: "I noticed that when I complimented you, you seem to have coupled it with criticism. What do you think that might be about?" We were able to process that most compliments in her family-of-origin were followed by criticism. Consequently, the compliment triggered the client, as she anticipated it being followed by hurtful criticism.

This had been a problematic theme in the client's relationships. One of the client's presenting problems was feeling invalidated and unappreciated by her family. I made a self-involving statement, describing an inclination to now be cautious with compliments (like her family), due to her reaction. The client recognized that her response kept her from getting what she wanted the most, which is validation and support. By acknowledging that the client's response was reasonable in light of her history, the client could identify a pattern of eliciting maneuvers (pairing compliments with criticisms) that evoked this undesired response from others. In a short period of time, a life-time pattern had been extinguished. We had discovered a skeleton key.

There is likely a reader noting that what's being described is Object Relations Theory (as cited in Simran, 2022), and the reader would be correct. However, traditional dynamic therapies often take years, and most therapists operate on short-term, "evidence-based" models. When the transition from more dynamic modalities occurred, it took some time to recognize what had been lost. Most veteran therapists already had a foundation in dynamic principles, so they were able to integrate new (more present-focused) models with an existing understanding of the relational dynamics. New therapists however appear to be missing the relational foundation.

Chapter 3: The Relational Chart®

T he Relational Chart® is my compromise solution. It enables the therapist to obtain enough information to effectively predict and respond to dynamics likely to impact the therapeutic relationship and ultimately therapeutic outcomes. It does not require a shift from the therapist's current orientation, but instead provides an important additional tool when problems arise in therapy. It is a simple tool that can be utilized to form working hypotheses. *Think of it as an insurance policy against empathic failure.*

Simple Definitions for the Relational Chart®:

Template (Bowlby, 1958): A template is like a jello mold. You pour liquid jello into the jello mold, and get the same shaped jello every time.

People have templates (molds) that consist of early childhood experiences, such as your relationship with your parents, siblings, institutions, etc. It's where we learn what "normal" is. During the creation of this template, there are positive and negative experiences, as well as misinformation, based on the age of the template creation. For example, if a four-year-old's parents get divorced, the child may assume (due to developmentally appropriate egocentrism) that it's their fault. An adult would intellectually understand that a divorce is never a child's fault, but the template was created with this misinformation. It's quite possible to see a 40-year-old client who still believes (consciously or unconsciously) that their parents' divorce was their fault. Object Relations therapists might use the term "introject" instead of a template (Simran, 2022).

Pattern (Simran, 2022): The pattern is the reenactment of the template. Unless there is challenge and/or intervention, the template will continue to produce the same jello (outcomes), no matter what life experiences are poured into the mold.

Relationship 1	Relationship 2	Relationship 3

For example, when you speak with survivors of domestic violence, there is almost always a pattern of these types of relationships. When they begin to recover, you might notice a shift from physically violent to emotionally abusive relationships, before entering a healthy relationship. These templates are etched into our psyche, so recovery is usually a gradual process, instead of a discrete episode.

Eliciting Maneuvers (Teyber, 2000): How we get others to behave in a predictable way, or fit into our mold. Read the definition again, as it's the concept that seems most elusive to therapists and clients; yet, it is key to breaking the pattern. In the above example, the client (Sarah) responded to compliments with defensiveness. This is an eliciting maneuver. By becoming defensive and confrontational, people are unlikely to repeat that behavior (complimenting her), leaving the client confused and invalidated. When some clients are triggered, they may become challenging and evocative. I'm reminded of the client who challenged my credentials, when we began discussing his destructive relationship with his sons. The client's challenging behavior was an eliciting maneuver designed to shut-down an uncomfortable (likely shame-producing) line of questioning. Of course, this client complained that nobody in his family was willing to discuss the situation with his sons. The client honestly didn't recognize that his reaction created the shut-down. Think of eliciting maneuvers as a self-fulfilling prophecy.

Pathogenic Beliefs (Teyber, 2000): Beliefs that keep the template in reenactment, or recipes that keep producing the same jello. Much of this occurs on an unconscious level. The client may believe that everyone holds their pathogenic beliefs. Think of the previously cited examples. Sarah believes that all compliments would contain a hidden insult, so she reacts accordingly. The domestic violence client may believe that all men are abusive, so they won't seek or expect anything else. Some other examples are as follows: "You have to have money (or be thin) to be loved." "All men (women) cheat." "People don't stand up for me, because I'm too sensitive." "All men (women) are jealous and competitive." "Get them, before they get you." "People will exploit you if you're vulnerable."

Core Belief (Beck, 1995): What does this pattern say about me, my value, my worth, etc.? *It's the center of the therapeutic onion.* If I believe I must have money to be loved, what does that say about me? (I'm unlovable.) If I must sustain abuse to be in a relationship, what does that say about my worth? (I'm unworthy.)

The following simplistic example is offered for clarity and practice. Karla is a 30-year-old Caucasian female who comes to therapy for depression, "because I can't keep a man." Karla reports that her father left when she was 6 years old and never returned. Karla has experienced three significant romantic relationships: one in high school, another in college and a marriage that resulted in divorce. Karla tearfully and sincerely asks, "Why do they all leave me? What's wrong with me?" Upon asking clarifying questions about the dissolution of these relationships, the therapist can filter through justifications, emotionalism, and lack of self-awareness and discover the following eliciting maneuvers that predicted abandonment: Karla cheated on her boyfriend in high school; her boyfriend in college was married, and her ex-husband had been married 4x before, never for longer than 6 months.

Let's apply this case to the Relational Chart®.

Template: Father leaves.

Pattern: Boyfriend in high school leaves. Boyfriend in college leaves. Husband leaves.

Eliciting Maneuver: She cheated on the boyfriend in high school. The boyfriend in college is married. Her husband has been married 4x before.

Pathogenic Belief: All men leave.

Core Belief: I am unlovable.

Template	Pattern	Eliciting Maneuver	Pathogenic Belief	Core Belief
Karla's father left.	Boyfriend in high school leaves. Boyfriend in college leaves. Husband leaves.	She cheated. He was married. 4 prior marriages	All men leave.	I am unlovable.

As you can see by Karla's example, an unexamined life often becomes a self-fulfilling prophecy. Consider how Karla's dynamics might surface in the therapeutic relationship. For example, you're a male therapist working with Karla utilizing thought records to challenge her pathogenic beliefs. Karla has missed several sessions and never returned her homework. Today's therapist (with little to no training in relational dynamics) may dismissively call this client non-compliant or "resistant". Based on her history however, what are her likely expectations of you? The relationship? How much effort will she put into the relationship, when she believes you will eventually leave too? Is it possible that not doing homework and missing sessions are eliciting maneuvers for termination (abandonment)? Is it possible that Karla views (consciously or unconsciously) using thought records as a distancing maneuver by you or rejection of her desire to have someone hear her pain? This conversation that needs to occur to evoke therapeutic change; otherwise, empathic failure (and premature termination) is eminent, as this is just another relationship that reinforces her belief that all men leave.

Allow me to provide another example of the importance of understanding basic relational dynamics at the onset of therapy. Carl is a 40-year-old, African American male who came to therapy at the insistence of his new wife, Katie. Carl reported feeling angry and depressed, as his children from marriage number two are often "mean" to Katie when they visit. Carl and Katie met at work, and this relationship appears to have factored into the divorce, but Carl is reluctant to acknowledge this. Carl's therapist is a 40-year-old divorced Latina, raising two children independently. As she listens to Carl's upset over the children's rejection of wife number three, she can't help but think, "Everything is about him. He doesn't seem to empathize with his former wife or their kids. What about the kids' feelings?!" Being a self-aware therapist, she could recognize countertransference and her interpretation was not verbalized. The therapist stated, "I can certainly see that this is impacting you. I'm wondering how you think the children might be experiencing this?" Carl became defensive, although he didn't know why. Carl responded, "I'm sorry, but I'm not one of those lib-er-al parents who lets the kids run the show." The therapist thinks, "So now I'm a touchy-feely lib-er-al for caring about your kids' feelings? Oh, I forgot it's all about YOU!" While the therapist is not overtly stating her feelings, the tension in the air is thick! Without appropriate intervention, Carl will not return to therapy as he will feel invalidated, and the therapist may secretly feel relieved that she won't have to deal with a "narcissistic" client.

What if the therapist had taken the time to complete the Relational Chart® at intake? How could a basic understanding of Carl's relational dynamics improved this exchange and likely prevented premature termination?

Through completing a Relational Chart® at intake, Carl's therapist discovered the following: Carl is a 40-year-old, African American male who came to therapy at the insistence of his wife, Katie. Carl reported being raised in a large, urban city by his mother; His father was in and out of prison his entire life. Carl stated that his mother remarried when he was 14 years of age. Carl and the stepfather did not get along, so Carl reported "sofa surfing" until he was 18 years old and joined the military. Carl has been married three times and has six children (three with wife number one, two with wife number two, and one in his current marriage). Carl stated that he met his first wife while stationed overseas, and she and the three children still live overseas, so he rarely sees them. Marriage number two ended with many animosities, as infidelity with Carl's current wife was a factor in the divorce. Carl stated that he has a hard time visiting with his children with wife number two, as they are unkind to Katie and if things don't change, he will end visits altogether. Katie is concerned about Carl's depression regarding the visits.

Let's place this limited information into the Relational Chart® and see what working hypotheses can be generated.

What is Carl's **template**? We know his father wasn't there consistently and that at the age of 14, he had to leave his mother's home, because he didn't get along with his stepfather. Carl likely internalized that mother chose the relationship with stepfather over a relationship with him.

What working hypotheses can we explore regarding Carl's **pattern**? There will likely be a history of relationship instability and abandonment. Carl's first wife and children have been abandoned the same way his father abandoned him. Infidelity with wife number two (eliciting abandonment) and threatening to end visitation if the kids are not "nice" to Katie, reenacts Carl's mother invalidating his feelings and choosing the stepfather over him.

Based on this information, what working hypotheses can we explore regarding Carl's **eliciting maneuvers**? Carl may unconsciously participate in behavior that elicits abandonment. He may be drawn to women who are less likely to be available emotionally or otherwise. He married someone whose home is overseas, so limited interaction following a divorce could be predicted. Infidelity in the second marriage (not surprisingly) elicited abandonment. Refusing to listen to his children's pain over his choices and expecting acceptance and compliance regardless of their feelings will elicit rejection and abandonment.

What working hypotheses can we explore regarding Carl's **pathogenic beliefs**? Fathers are unimportant. Men leave. The feelings of children are unimportant. If relationships become challenging, abandonment is an option.

What working hypotheses can we explore regarding Carl's **core beliefs**? (If my dad left me and my mom left me), I must not be lovable or important.

Template	Pattern	Eliciting Maneuver	Pathogenic Belief	Core Belief
Father wasn't in his life consistently. Mother abandoned the client, and choose his stepfather over him.	Client is not involved with children from his first marriage. Client is threatening to abandon children from marriage number two over stepmother.	Married someone who lives overseas. Infidelity and abandonment of family number two. Lacking empathy for the children's perspective.	Fathers are unimportant. The feelings children are unimportant. Parenting is optional.	I am unlovable and unimportant.

These working hypotheses can be supported (or not) through exploration, but you get the point. Let's try the session again, with the therapist knowing Carl's internal working model.

Carl is a 40-year-old, African American male who came to therapy at the insistence of his new wife, Katie. Carl reported feeling angry and depressed, as his children from marriage number two are often "mean" to Katie when they visit. Carl and Katie met at work, and this relationship factored into the divorce. Carl's therapist is a 40-year-old divorced Latina, raising two children independently. As she listens to Carl's upset over the children's rejection of wife number three, she can't help but think, "Everything is about him. He doesn't seem to empathize with his former wife or their kids, **but** this makes perfect sense based on his background. It seems that he's invalidating the kids the same way he was invalidated." Being an insightful therapist, she understands that if she can get Carl in touch with his invalidated pain, and provide a corrective emotional experience through validating his pain, he will likely be able to do the same for his children. The therapist states, "You know Carl, as I'm listening to your frustration over the relationship between your kids and Katie, I couldn't help but wonder what it must have been like to be a 14-

year-old boy, "sofa surfing" because he didn't get along with his stepfather."

A basic understanding of the client's internal working model changed therapy from combative to compassionate and problem-centered to person-centered. At this point, I suspect that at least one new therapist is asking, "Why do I need to know all of this? Couldn't I address the visitation issue, focus on exceptions to the negative visits and build upon this?" No. Look at what happened in the first exchange when the therapist addressed only the symptoms. The underlying relational dynamics destroyed any real possibility of continued therapy. Regardless of orientation, you need to understand relational dynamics enough to overcome any interference with your therapy goals.

Chapter 4: Your Turn

The Case of Ralph

Ralph is a 50-year-old Caucasian male who has come to therapy for depression. Ralph is a high-profile businessman who has appeared in magazines and newspapers with various young models on his arm. Ralph says that he longs for a serious relationship and is ready to settle down, but "I always end up with gold diggers." Ralph's father was a plumber by trade with few career aspirations. Ralph's mother, Rita, left Ralph's father when he was seven years old for a successful surgeon who was kind to him, but a "total womanizer", a fact Rita will not acknowledge. Ralph reported missing his father terribly and trying to encourage him to succeed, so "We can go home". Ralph said, "I grew to resent him (dad) for not even trying, but I resented her (mom) more. My dad died two years ago, alone. He never got over her. She's had more plastic surgery than Joan Rivers and is still the belle of the ball at the country club. Thanks to Viagra, my stepfather is still a womanizer. Still, it seems to work for them." Ralph reported dating many exciting and glamourous women for brief periods, but "when the money dries up, so does the love". He reported that he once dated a school teacher who became a good friend, but "I just wasn't attracted to her. She isn't into the lifestyle."

Describe Ralph's template.

Describe any repetition of the template or patterns.

What do you suspect could be Ralph's eliciting maneuvers (or how he gets others to behave predictably)?

What do you suspect are Ralph's pathogenic beliefs?

What do you suspect are Ralph's core beliefs?

Complete Ralph's Relational Chart®

Template	Pattern	Eliciting Maneuver	Pathogenic Belief	Core Belief

Let's review together.

Describe Ralph's **template**. Mother left father for a more successful man. Ralph blamed his father (partly) for a lack of ambition that (in Ralph's mind) would have otherwise reunified the family. Ralph's stepfather was kind to him, but a womanizer.

Describe any repetition of the template or **patterns**. Ralph is successful like his stepfather and appears to be a womanizer. He dated several exciting and glamourous women (like mom) for brief periods, "but when the money dries up, so does the love."

What do you suspect could be Ralph's **eliciting maneuvers** (or how he gets others to behave in a predictable way)? Ralph appears to be drawn to the same superficial type of women (like mom) and rejects women who may have the capacity for something more substantial.

What do you suspect are Ralph's **pathogenic beliefs**? "All women are superficial gold diggers." "When the money dries up, so does the love." "Women who genuinely like me are undesirable."

What do you suspect are Ralph's **core beliefs**? (I must have money to be loved, or if you genuinely like me, there's something wrong with you), because "I am unlovable." Ralph's Relational Chart®

Template	Pattern	Eliciting Maneuver	Pathogenic Belief	Core Belief
Mother left dad for money. Dad was unmotivated and therefore, abandoned. Stepfather was a successful, womanizer.	Ralph became a successful, womanizer.	Attracted to superficial women. Rejecting women with the capacity of something more.	To be loved, you must have money. If you genuinely like me, there must be something wrong with you.	I am unlovable.

How did you do? It's more of an art than a science, especially with such limited information. Let's explore how Ralph's internal working model could interfere with therapy.

For the male therapists:

You are in the early stages of therapy with Ralph, but you seem to be progressing towards a positive working alliance. You ask, "Ralph, I'm wondering if your selection of women (exciting and glamourous) might be impacting your ability to form the meaningful relationship you want." Ralph abruptly replies, "Everybody wants a model. Even you want a model, but you can't have one, so you settled for this. Don't you want something more?!"

For the female therapists:

You are in the early stages of therapy with Ralph, but you seem to be progressing towards a positive working alliance. You ask, "Ralph, I'm wondering if your selection of women (exciting and glamourous) might be impacting your ability to form the meaningful relationship you want." Ralph abruptly replies, "Everybody wants to be a model. Even you want to be a model, but you can't, so you settled for this. Don't you want something more?"

What happened? Ralph's responses are uncharacteristically evocative, and it's only human to feel perhaps a bit defensive. You know what you asked, but based on Ralph's response...that's not what he heard. Statements like these are designed to elicit a response. In these instances, a process comment is often helpful. "Ralph, I asked you if your selection of partners maybe impacting your ability to have the type of relationship you want. Your response was to challenge me. What do think that's about? What did you hear me suggesting in that question?" Ralph replies, "No good woman would want me." The therapist's question regarding his relationship choices triggered shame and defensiveness. We can explore this further based on your knowledge of Ralph's internal working model.

Ralph may attempt to fit his therapist into his internal working model. The male therapist is likely a father representation. This is especially evident in his question, "Don't you want something more?!" Ralph could never get his father to aspire to Rita's definition of success and consequently, Ralph's family dissolved. For Ralph, there are two ways to be a man: successful and exploitative OF women or less inspired and exploited BY women. Understanding this dynamic should help to develop questions like, "Ralph, you're asking me if I want something more. Is it possible that I am happy with what I have? Is it possible that your father was happy with what he had? Could it be that *you* want something more?"

Ralph may also try to fit a female therapist into his internal working model. Remember that all women are gold diggers, or they are the undesirable matronly types. For Ralph, there are two ways to be a woman: exciting, glamourous and exploitative OF men or plain or substantial and exploited BY men. There is no frame of reference for an attractive and substantial woman. Based on the mother's behavior, Ralph is anticipating that you too will want more. Some beneficial questions (like the following) may help to elicit further discussion, "Ralph, you're asking me if I want something more. Mother had more money, but that doesn't necessarily mean more love and happiness. What was the price you paid so she could have more? Could it be *you* that want something more than she had?"

Let's imagine that we're now preparing for termination with Ralph. You have intervened on many destructive patterns and assisted him in identifying his eliciting maneuvers. Ralph began dating his teacher friend again, as he finds her much more attractive now. Ralph is automatically challenging his pathogenic beliefs and core beliefs. The following scenario could apply to either a male or female therapist and demonstrates how dynamics can impact even termination.

As you and Ralph prepare for termination, Ralph makes the following job offer: "I think you're a wonderful therapist and would be an amazing asset to my company. I know you can't work for me until we terminate, but when we do, I am willing to offer you $500,000 a year to create and implement an Employee Assistance Program (EAP). I think we would be an incredible team." With your understanding of Ralph's internal working model, what do you suspect is going on?

Ralph (on some level) still thinks he needs to buy people's love and connection, or at least, it is still an automatic thought. For the male therapist, it would be like dad finally seeking success, so "We can go home." For the female therapist, Ralph believes the best way to keep a woman in his life is through money. So obviously this job offer (while possibly tempting) would be completely inappropriate. At this point in the relationship, a comment like, "I'm very flattered, but I am wondering if you're scared of losing this relationship and trying to buy me into staying? I care about you and feel the loss, but I also recognize that you don't need to have a relationship with a therapist to meet your needs. You have everything inside of you to maintain a nurturing, successful relationships that you don't have to pay for."

The Case of Maria

Maria is a 35-year-old, Latina. Her parents immigrated from Mexico when they were young adults. Growing up, Maria's parents were farm workers who only spoke Spanish. Consequently, she translated exchanges between her parents and the world (e.g., landlords, teachers, police, etc.). Maria noted that her parents were often wrong, when she went to them for advice. They didn't understand how things worked in America and the more educated she became, the more glaring the differences were. Maria's siblings often came to her instead of her parents for advice. Maria went to college and became an excellent social worker. Despite this, Maria has difficulty maintaining employment, and is coming to therapy, as she's afraid that she won't pass probation at her new job. Maria reported that she struggles to get along with supervisors. She reports that her current supervisor doesn't have the same credentials, although they are considered professionally equivalent. Maria doesn't feel like her boss knows what she's talking about. Maria states, "I try to educate her, but she gets mad. The other trainees turn to me for advice… that's not my fault!"

Using the limited information in the vignette, create a Relational Chart® for Maria.

Template	Pattern	Eliciting Maneuver	Pathogenic Belief	Core Belief

Your chart should be similar to the one presented below although these are only working hypotheses, so differences are acceptable too.

Template	Pattern	Eliciting Maneuver	Pathogenic Belief	Core Belief
Parents are non-English speaking immigrants. Maria had responsibilities and authority inconsistent with the child's status. Her siblings came to her for advices, not the parents.	Maria tries to assume an authority position inconsistent with her status. Peers come to her for advice,	She does not respect the expertise of her supervisors and challenges them. She overestimates her expertise, and peers are drawn to her persona, not her expertise.	I am responsible for the success of my family. Authority figures always be right, or they can't be trusted. I can't trust anyone, but myself.	(I must be right), or I am a failure. I am alone.

Let's examine how Maria's internal working model might manifest in therapy. Warning: This example contains countertransference propensities or is reality-based. The therapist listens carefully and empathically to Maria's story, while internally empathizing with the supervisors of this "know-it-all" trainee. The therapist challenges Maria by asking, "Is it possible that your supervisors have something to teach you? While it is true that supervisors can be wrong too, is it possible that they are reacting negatively to you, because you invalidate their experiences and expertise?" Maria replies, "Maybe, but I don't think you understand. Where did you say you went to school? Is it APA accredited?" The therapist begrudgingly provided Maria with the requested information. Maria does not return to therapy, and the therapist is grateful.

Now, let's try this exchange again utilizing the information we obtained from the Relational Chart®. The therapist can expect to be challenged by this client, not due to some annoying superiority complex, but due to the client's anxiety over being wrong. Remember, the client feels responsible for the entire family's success (or failure), so the price of being wrong is high. It is strongly speculated that Maria's authority figures have been wrong in a way that produced humiliation and other negative consequences. While her parents certainly wanted to be helpful and offer advice, Maria always had to weigh their information against the language barrier and the often-nuanced policies and procedures in the United States. The therapist might begin by asking, "I'm wondering what it's cost you in the past, when authority figures were wrong?" The therapist should also advise Maria that the therapist will be wrong and likely unintentionally fail her at some point. When this happens, how might we handle it?

In other words, the therapist is planting the seeds of a corrective emotional experience. The therapist is an authority figure and will be wrong. Can we salvage the relationship? Can a person be both highly credible and wrong from time to time? What did Maria do with the anger (and fear) over not having parents to turn to for answers? Is Maria denying herself the connectedness and support of a supervisor by prematurely discounting their knowledge? Is Maria okay with being wrong and when she is wrong, what does she tell herself about this?

These exercises should strongly illustrate the importance of understanding relational dynamics in therapy. You don't need to grow a beard or acquire a German accent to use this information in even, brief solution-focused therapies. You just need to know enough to conceptualize and intervene upon dynamics that may interfere with your client reaching their goals.

This intervention is not inconsistent with your current orientation. The chart will illustrate well-known dynamic conceptualizations, if you practice Psychodynamic, Object Relations and / or Bowenian therapy. If you practice Cognitive-Behavioral therapy, challenging pathogenic and core beliefs is part of your orientation (Beck, 1995). If you practice solution-focused therapy, the chart will illustrate previously attempted solutions and meaning-making (Miller, 2019). If you practice Acceptance and Commitment Therapy (ACT), you will identify the pattern of avoidance evident in the eliciting maneuvers (Moore, 2019). If you're a Dialectical Behavior Therapist (DBT), the chart will help identify eliciting maneuvers and beliefs triggering emotional dysregulation (Tanning, 2019). Of course, these are but a few examples.

Not investing in understanding the dynamics of the therapeutic relationship can have dire consequences for the client. Therapy is supposed to be about the client, not what is convenient or simple for us to understand. Being a therapist comes with a moral and ethical obligation to do no harm. If you're practicing without this understanding, you have likely harmed and will continue to do so. It's inevitable.

Chapter 5: The Other Component of the Therapeutic Relationship

This section separates the professionals from the amateurs. Up to this point, we have been discussing how the client's internal working model can impact therapy. Of equal (if not greater importance), is recognition of the therapist's internal working model and how it impacts your ability to provide competent therapy. Part of some student capstone presentations are discussions of countertransference. I always shudder when a student reports "no countertransference" in any case.

Countertransference comes with having a pulse. You come to the profession with your own templates, patterns, eliciting maneuvers, and pathogenic and core beliefs. A student once told me, "Yes, but I don't let countertransference get in the way of my doing good therapy." How do you know? Isn't your conceptualization of "good therapy" based on your template and beliefs? The following brief questionnaire should assist you in identifying but a few of your human biases:

1. My stance on abortion is_____.
2. My political affiliation is _____.
3. Should mother's work outside of the home? Yes / No
4. Should homosexuals be able to adopt children? Yes / No
5. My religious preference is _____.

6. Parents should be able to receive supplemental income, if their child has been diagnosed with Attention-Deficit / Hyperactivity Disorder? Yes / No
7. Psychotropic medications are appropriate for children. Yes / No
8. Being raised in a polygamist home damages children psychologically. Yes / No
9. Transgenderism is more political than physiological. Yes / No

As previously stated, countertransference comes with having a pulse…and a brain. Look at your response to any of these questions, and the potential impact on therapy should be obvious. For example, while you would likely know enough to not express to a pregnant teenager your prolife position overtly, the discussion's direction (often unconsciously) may be impacted, especially if you're passionate about the issue.

As a therapist we cannot pretend not to have personal biases and countertransference; rather, we must be aware of it and take steps to mitigate the possible damage to the therapeutic relationship. Unfortunately, people are often unaware of their most glaring character defects, and being a therapist is the greatest defense mechanism of all. Our assessment of our strengths and weaknesses is filtered through self-bias. Some therapists are so unaware that they assume premature termination is mostly about the client's resistance, instead of exploring what they may or may not be doing to elicit this response. Who is the common denominator?

If through fear and/or a lack of humility, you choose not to explore your dynamics in a meaningful way, please reconsider… because you will hurt people. As an ethical therapist, self-awareness is not optional. Empathic failure is almost always the result of a lack of awareness by the therapist. After feeling misunderstood and/or invalidated by the therapist, a client may never return. It often takes years for someone to become so desperate that they seek therapy in the first place, and your lack of awareness may be their final straw. Self-awareness is not optional.

I have designed worksheets to assist therapists in recognizing their internal working models. (This, of course, could also be used with high functioning clients.) This method was first used in group supervision experiences, as many therapists struggled with these concepts. Many interns (associates) continue to note that it is one of the most powerful and enlightening supervisory exercises they have experienced. The facilitator will also learn so much more about themselves. I would recommend doing this in a small group supervision setting. However, if the group is not close or interpersonally safe, I would suggest either doing this with your mentor/ supervisor, or a small group of trusted friends / colleagues. To gain an understanding (prior to facilitating), *I strongly recommend you do these exercises yourself, first*. You can't give somebody something you don't have, nor can you successfully teach something that isn't meaningful to you.

Utilized the following directions to facilitate this experience:

1. Select a designated day and time each week for your group meeting. There should be no more than six group members, and each meeting should be two hours long. Each group member will need a **large** piece of poster or tag board for their Relational Chart®.

Template	Pattern	Eliciting Maneuver	Pathogenic Belief	Core Belief

2. Explain to the group the purpose of these exercises and that some of the information may be evocative. Each member has a choice regarding the depth of information shared, from superficial to very personal. Like most things in life however, each group member will get out of the exercises, exactly what they put into it.

3. Group members will not share their worksheets with the group. The worksheets are done privately, so members do not need to be concerned with sharing the content or producing a "right answer". Each member will bring their Relational Chart® (a summation of the worksheets) to group. Again, this allows each group member an opportunity to share as much or as little as they are comfortable with.

4. Complete the worksheet labeled "Finding Your Template" (Appendix A, page 75). Take your time. I recommend completing one worksheet per week; otherwise, the assignment will likely become overwhelming, and you won't benefit from it. Once you have finished the worksheet, go to "The Key to the Relational Chart" (Appendix F, page 116) and place each of your responses from the questionnaire under the designated heading or subheading of the Relational Chart.

The Relational Chart®: Template Example

Template	Pattern	Pathogenic Belief
Demographics Bayfield, Maine (0-12) Safe, Independent Play Walter, Nevada (12+) Middle Class Parents – Married 50 years Oldest Child		
Female Authority Figure Anger- Yelled, cried, overate, demeaning, won. Sad-Overate, cried, isolate Joy – neighborhood mom, creative, recovery, funny. Work – Fired a lot Compete – Dad's loyalty even when she was wrong, appearances.		
Male Authority Figure Anger-peacekeeper with mom even at our expense Sad-Isolates, work more		

Joy-Listener, outdoors, Gets along with everyone Work – Dedicated Loved, but unclear about respect of spouse. Failure to protect.		
<u>Peers</u> Brother – Talented athlete, likable, popular, extended family preference, poor academics, told my secrets, unsupportive, victim postures. Friends – Exclusivity. One best friend. Some betrayal, but Mostly positive and supportive.		
<u>Culture</u> Religion – Baptist, God was to be feared. Ethnicity – Caucasian, French, and American. Middle Class Expectations – Get married and have children Racism – Told that it was bad, but no recognition of white privilege.		

5. The facilitator should assess the group's readiness to move onto the next topic, patterns. That is, some groups are very matter-of-fact about the template exercise, while others enjoy sharing stories and emotions, and either is fine based on the group dynamic. However, do not let the discussion of templates exceed one (two-hour) meeting. Facilitators want to promote awareness and general discussion, not conduct group therapy. Obviously, this exercise can be evocative for some, and may warrant additional discussion with a particular member, excusal from the activity, or possibly referrals.

Finding Your Patterns

1. Complete the questionnaire labeled "Finding Your Patterns" (Appendix B, page 83). Take your time. Use" The Key to the Relational Chart" (Appendix F, page 116) to identify which item number belongs under which heading. Underline any similarities found between the template and the pattern.

The Relational Chart®: Pattern Example

Template	Pattern
Demographics Bayfield, Maine (0-12) Safe, Independent Play Walter, Nevada (12+) Middle Class Parents – Married 50 years Oldest Child	Demographics Walter, Nevada Safe, but isolated Little Independent Play Upper Middle Class Married for 22 years Two moves within the city
Female Authority Figure Anger- Yelled, cried, overate, demeaning, won. Sad-Overate, cried, isolate Joy – neighborhood mom, creative, recovery, funny. Work – Fired a lot Compete – Dad's loyalty even when she was wrong, appearances.	Female Authority Figures Teachers – Loving, felt special, fair, Humiliation Bosses – Overall loving & fair, but occasionally competitive undermining-feel misjudged / helpless Work – Hero. Hard-working and dedicated.
Male Authority Figure Anger-peacekeeper with mom even at our expense Sad-Isolates, work more Joy-Listener, outdoors, Gets along with everyone Work – Dedicated Loved, but unclear about respect of spouse. Failure to protect.	Male Authority Figures Teachers – Mix. Favorite on one occasion and rejected at the next. Bosses – Overall kind and fair, but can be passive and not advocating when I need it.

Peers Brother – Talented athlete, likable, popular, extended family preference, poor academics, told my secrets, unsupportive, victim postures. Friends – Exclusivity. One best friend. Some betrayal.	Peers Exclusivity. One true friend. Many acquaintances. Positives-shared experiences and connection. Negatives- told my secrets. Few betrayals. Mostly positive
Culture Religion – Baptist, God was to be feared. Ethnicity – Caucasian, French, and American. Middle Class Expectations – Get married and have children Racism – Told that it was bad, but no recognition of white privilege.	Culture Religion – Spiritual, God is to be loved. Ethnicity – Caucasian-America Subculture – LGBTQ family Stereotypes – must have been given everything, not curvy or appealing. Racism – Taught kids to be aware of white privilege.
Blank for Template	Romance 1st -Communicative, funny, unfaithful, addiction, lies, manipulation and abuse. 2nd – Loyal and kind. Surface Communication (some loneliness). Both find meaning in work.
Blank for Template	Children Anger – Irritable, isolating, Sad – Crying, isolating Spouse Anger – Sarcasm Spouse Sad – Void Joy – Spending time together, crafts, travel, special moments

2. Each group member should bring their Relational Chart® to group and share their discoveries to the extent of each member's comfort level. If anyone struggles to find similarities, the facilitator and group members can be very helpful. Remember, similarities are not always as blatant as "my father drank, and my husband drinks". It can be "My father drank when anxious, and I overeat when anxious" or the similarity is substance abuse in reaction to anxiety. Note in the example similarities in life style, and relationships. Ask the group if there were any revelations.

3. The facilitator should assess the group's readiness to move onto the next topic, eliciting maneuvers. Some groups are very matter-of-fact about the pattern exercise, while others enjoy sharing stories and emotions, and either is fine based on the group dynamic. However, do not let the discussion of patterns exceed one (two-hour) meeting. Remember, the goal is to promote awareness.

Finding Your Eliciting Maneuvers

1. The next set of worksheets is a bit different. The focus has been on patterns and many things about "other people". If we ever hope to grow, we must have humility. Some people equate "humility" with "humiliation" which is not the case. Humility allows us to self-reflect with the expectation that we contribute to our problems. "I did _____, because he/she did _____" is as far as many people get concerning their own accountability, and this approach is disempowering and lacks insight. Our reactions belong to us. Think about how a person could respond to a stranger confronting them in the store (fight, flight, or freeze); it depends on the person. This is not intended to be shame-inducing or victim-blaming, but to build awareness, so you have more power in your relationships and in your ability to respond to clients' eliciting maneuvers. Complete the questionnaire labeled "Finding Your Eliciting Maneuvers" (Appendix C, page 94). Take your time. Use

the "Key to the Relational Chart" (Appendix F, page 116) to identify which item number belongs under which heading. Underline any of your eliciting maneuvers that likely evoked (caused) the reactions noted in the patterns.

Relational Chart®: Eliciting Maneuver Example:

Template	Pattern	Eliciting Maneuvers
Demographics Bayfield, Maine (0-12) Safe, Independent Play Walter, Nevada (12+) Middle Class Parents – Married 50 years Oldest Child	Demographics Walter, Nevada Safe, but isolated Little Independent Play Upper Middle Class Married for 22 years Two moves within the city	Demographics College and Two Jobs Husband is employed Stayed in Walter for Family Upper Middle Class Stayed Married
Female Authority Figure Anger- Yelled, cried, overate, demeaning, won. Sad-Overate, cried, isolate Joy – neighborhood mom, creative, recovery, funny. Work – Fired a lot Compete – Dad's loyalty even when	Female Authority Figures Teachers – Loving, felt special, fair, Humiliation Bosses – Overall loving & fair, but occasionally competitive undermining-feel misjudged / helpless Work – Hero. Hard-working and dedicated.	Female Authority Figures Guilty until proven innocent. Anxious, defensive & afraid. I must prove myself. Hypervigilant to invalidation or competitiveness. Helpless and dismayed or arrogant and defensive. Dichotomous

she was wrong, appearances.		classification: Perfect Mother or Monster.
Male Authority Figure Anger-peacekeeper with mom even at our expense Sad-Isolates, work more Joy-Listener, outdoors, Gets along with everyone Work – Dedicated Loved, but unclear about respect of spouse. Failure to protect.	Male Authority Figures Teachers – Mix. Favorite on one occasion and rejected at the next. Bosses – Overall kind and fair, but can be passive and not advocating when I need it.	Male Authority Figures I have always given benefit of the doubt. Aim to please. Expect loyalty and advocacy. Ignore and/or rationalize invalidating behavior or signs of a lack of loyalty. Assume their behavior is my fault.
Peers Brother – Talented athlete, likable, popular, extended family preference, poor academics, told my secrets, unsupportive, victim postures. Friends – Exclusivity. One best friend. Some betrayal, but Mostly positive and supportive.	Peers Exclusivity. One true friend. Many acquaintances. Positives-shared experiences and connection. Negatives-told my secrets. Few betrayals.	Peers Exclusivity. Giving everything to 1-2 friends - can be harsh with high expectations. Lack of investment and/or neglectful/ dismissive of others.

Culture	Culture	Culture
Religion – Baptist, God was to be feared. (Continued on next page) Ethnicity – Caucasian, French, and American. Middle Class Expectations – Get married and have children Racism – Told that it was bad, but no recognition of white privilege.	Religion – Spiritual, God is to be loved. (Continued on next page) Ethnicity – Caucasian-America Subculture – LGBTQ family Stereotypes – must have been given everything, not curvy or appealing. Racism – Taught kids to be aware of white privilege.	Often neglect spiritual matters unless desperate. Assume that some rejection comes from my Ethnicity. Hurt that it's socially acceptable to mock or belittle my culture – double standard. No group is superior, and the rules should be the same.
Blank for Template	Romance 1st -Communicative, funny, unfaithful, addiction, lies, manipulation and abuse. 2nd – Loyal and kind. Surface Communication (some loneliness). Both find meaning in work.	Romance Bait & Switch – my issues 1st – Tolerated unacceptable behavior, desperate, and devalued. 2nd – Ignore problems (lazy & easily frustrated), neglect relationship, work to avoid emptiness.
Blank for Template	Children Anger – Irritable, isolating, Sad – Crying, isolating Spouse Anger – Sarcasm Spouse Sad – Void Joy – Spending time together, crafts, travel, special moments	Adult Children Very loving, but very distant. Anger & pain are not discussed; we don't want to hurt each other. Neglected relationship. Struggle with genuineness, but very generous.

2. Each group member should bring their Relational Chart® to group. Discussion of the eliciting maneuvers section is generally the most evocative, as we're talking about our own character defects, so the importance of interpersonal safety is paramount for effectiveness. Each group member may share about their eliciting maneuvers, and *if the group is interpersonally safe*, the presenter can ask for group feedback. This experience can be eye-opening and life-changing. People are often unaware that we are eliciting the same responses from coworkers and supervisors, as we do with outside relationships. Look at the example and note that most of the eliciting maneuvers are underlined, because our behavior directly predicts most patterns/outcomes.

Finding Your Pathogenic Beliefs

1. Complete the worksheet labeled "Finding Your Pathogenic Beliefs" on (Appendix D, page 107). Take your time. Use the Key to the Relational Chart (Appendix F, page 116) to identify which item number belongs under which heading. Underline the relationship between your eliciting maneuvers and pathogenic beliefs. For example, if your pathogenic belief is that "people will abandon you" your eliciting maneuver of "not allowing anyone to get close to you" is fairly predictive.

Relational Chart®: Pathogenic Beliefs Example

Eliciting Maneuver	Pathogenic Belief	Core Belief
Demographics College and Two Jobs Husband is employed Stayed in Walter for Family Upper Middle Class Stayed Married	Demographics If you don't work, you don't have value. Must stay married. Must live close to family, even if conflicted.	

Female Authority Figures Guilty until proven innocent. Anxious, defensive & afraid. must prove myself. Hypervigilant to invalidation or competitiveness. Helpless and dismayed or arrogant and defensive. Dichotomous classification Perfect Mother or Monster.	Female Authority Not trustworthy, until proven to be. I am helpless and you will bury me, if you feel threatened. You are either the perfect mother or a monster	
Male Authority Figures I have always given benefit of the doubt. I aim to please. Expect loyalty and advocacy. Ignore and/or rationalize invalidating behavior or signs of a lack of loyalty. Assume their behavior is my fault.	Male Authority If you hurt me, it's my fault. You will not protect me. You will betray me, despite my loyalty.	
Peers Exclusivity. Giving everything to 1-2 friends -can be harsh with high expectations. Lack of investment and/or neglectful/dismissive of others.	Peers Only invest in 1 or 2, or enough to survive. They take, take & take, then leave or betray you. Most are not worth the investment of time.	

Culture Often neglect spiritual matters unless desperate. Assume that some rejection comes from my Ethnicity. Hurt that it's socially acceptable to mock or belittle my culture – double standards. No group is superior, and the rules should be the same.	Culture With God, invest the minimum for survival and favor. Other cultures are not seeking equality, but superiority and payback. You will always be the bad guy.	
Romance Bait & Switch – my issues 1st – Tolerated unacceptable behavior, desperate, and devalued. 2nd– Ignore problems (lazy & easily frustrated), neglect relationship, work to avoid the emptiness.	Romance Men will pursue you until they get what they want, and you will be devalued. Men can take care of themselves, and don't need much attention.	
Adult Children Very loving, but very distant. Anger & pain are not discussed. We don't want to hurt each other. Neglected relationship. Struggle with genuineness, but very generous.	Adult Children My child is very fragile physically and emotionally and cannot withstand confrontation. She will reject me or yell at me, if I discuss my feelings.	

2. Each group member should bring their Relational Chart to the group. A direct link between eliciting maneuvers and pathogenic beliefs should be noted. The facilitator should encourage discussion about eliciting maneuvers likely to trigger your pathogenic beliefs and vice-versa. This is a good opportunity to review cognitive and mindfulness skills, and to discuss deliberate alternative responses. The facilitator should ask the group to reflect upon at least one occasion where their eliciting maneuvers and/or pathogenic beliefs negatively impacted therapy. If anyone cannot recognize a time when this occurred, greater self-reflection is needed. This again requires vulnerability, but awareness of this nature is a professional ethic.

Finding Your Core Beliefs

1. Complete the worksheet labeled "Finding Your Core Beliefs" (Appendix E, page 111). Take your time. Use "The Key to the Relational Chart" (Appendix F, page 116) to identify where to place items. Underline the similarities between your pathogenic beliefs and your core beliefs. An easy way to do this is to ask yourself, if my pathogenic belief is true, what does it say about me?

Relational Chart®: Core Beliefs Example:

Pathogenic Belief	Core Belief
Demographics If you don't work, you don't have value. Must stay married. Must live close to family, even if conflicted.	Demographics I am not lovable enough to be taken care of. You are not worth being treated with respect by family.

Female Authority Not trustworthy, until proven to be. I am helpless and you will bury me, if you feel threatened. You are either the perfect mother or a monster.	**Female Authority** You don't deserve success, because it makes others feel like less of a person.
Male Authority If you hurt me, it's my fault. You will not protect me. You will betray me, despite my loyalty.	**Male Authority** I am unworthy of being protected. I am unworthy of loyalty.
Peers Only invest in 1 or 2, or enough to survive. They take, take & take, then leave or betray you. Most are not worth the investment of time.	**Peers** I'm not loved for who I am, but for what I can give. Therefore, I am unlovable.
Culture With God, invest the minimum for survival and favor. Other cultures are not seeking equality, but superiority and payback. You will always be the bad guy.	**Culture** I am unimportant. I am unworthy of being treated with respect.
Romance Men will pursue you until they get what they want, then you will be devalued. Men can take care of themselves, and don't need much attention.	**Romance** I am expendable, to be used up and thrown away. He is unimportant.

Adult Children	Adult Children
My child is very fragile physically and emotionally and cannot withstand confrontation. She will reject me or yell at me, if I discuss my feelings.	I am a failure. I am a bad mother. My child doesn't love me.

2. Each group member should bring their Relational Chart to the group. The facilitator should encourage the group to discuss the impact of their core beliefs in personal relationships (if appropriate) and interaction with clients. Note times that you felt defensive, afraid, unworthy, unloved, and/or inferior in a therapeutic exchange. How can we identify (in the moment) that our knee-jerk reaction is likely due to countertransference, as opposed to something with the client? This again requires vulnerability, and a basic review of cognitive therapy skills is highly encouraged.

Example of a Completed Relational Chart:

Your chart will be on one large piece of paper or tag board.

Template	Pattern	Eliciting Maneuver	Pathogenic Belief	Core Belief
Demographics	Demographics	Demographics	Demographics	Demographics
Bayfield, Maine (0-12)	Walter, Nevada	College and Two Jobs	If you don't work, you don't have value. Must stay married. Must live close to family, even if conflicted.	I am not lovable enough to be taken care of. You are not worth being treated with respect by family.
Safe, Independent Play	Safe, but isolated	Husband is employed		
Walter, Nevada (12+)	Little Independent Play	Stayed in Walter for Family		
Middle Class	Upper Middle Class	Upper Middle Class		
Parents – Married 50 years	Married for 22 years	Stayed Married		
Oldest Child	Two moves within the city			
Female Authority Figure	Female Authority Figure	Female Authority Figure	Female Authority	Female Authority
Anger- Yelled, cried, overate, demeaning, won.		Guilty until proven innocent. Anxious, defensive & afraid. I must prove myself. Hypervigilant to invalidation or competitiveness. Helpless and dismayed or arrogant and defensive. Dichotomous classification: Perfect Mother or Monster.	Not trustworthy, until proven to be.	
Sad-Overate, cried, isolate	Teachers – Loving, felt special, fair, Humiliation			≡
Joy – neighborhood mom, creative, recovery, funny.	Bosses – Overall loving & fair, but occasionally competitive undermining- feel misjudged / helpless		I am helpless and you will bury me, if you feel threatened. You are either the perfect mother or a monster.	You don't deserve success, because it makes others feel like less of a person.
Work – Fired a lot				
Compete – Dad's loyalty even when she was wrong, appearances.	Work – Hero. Hard- working and dedicated.			

Template	Pattern	Eliciting Maneuver	Pathogenic Belief	Core Belief
Male Authority Figure A peacekeeper with mom even at our expense Sad-Isolates, work more Joy-Listener, outdoors, Gets along with everyone Work – Dedicated Loved, but unclear about respect of spouse. Failure to protect.	Male Authority Figures Teachers – Mix. Favorite on one occasion and rejected the next. Bosses – Overall kind and fair, but can be passive and not advocating when I need it.	Male Authority Figures Always given the benefit of the doubt. Aim to please. Expect loyalty and advocacy. Ignore and/or rationalize invalidating behavior or signs of a lack of loyalty. Assume their behavior is my fault.	Male Authority If you hurt me, it's my fault. You will not protect me. You will betray me, despite my loyalty.	Male Authority I am unworthy of being protected. I am unworthy of loyalty.
Peers Brother – Talented athlete, likable, popular, extended family preference, poor academics, told my secrets, unsupportive, victim postures. Friends – Exclusivity. One best friend. Some betrayal, but positive and supportive.	Peers Exclusivity. One true friend. Many acquaintances. Positives-shared experiences and connection. Negatives- told my secrets. Few betrayals.	Peers Exclusivity. Giving everything to 1-2 friends -can be harsh with high expectations. Lack of investment and/ Or neglectful/ dismissive of others.	Peers Only invest in 1 or 2, or enough to survive. They take, take & take, then leave or betray you. Most are not worth the investment of time.	Peers I'm not loved for who I am, but for what I can give. Therefore, I am unlovable.

18

Template	Pattern	Eliciting Maneuver	Pathogenic Belief	Core Belief
Culture	Culture	Culture	Culture	Culture
Religion – Baptist, God was to be feared. Ethnicity – Caucasian, French, and American. Middle Class Expectations – Get married and have children Racism – Told that it was bad, but no recognition of white privilege.	Religion – Spiritual, God is to be loved. Ethnicity – Caucasian America Subculture – LGBTQ family Stereotypes – must have been given everything, not curvy or appealing. Racism – Taught kids to be aware of white privilege.	Often neglect spiritual matters unless desperate. Assume that some rejection comes from my Ethnicity. Hurt that it's socially acceptable to mock or belittle my culture – double standard. No group is superior, and the rules should be the same.	With God, invest the minimum for survival and favor. Other cultures are not seeking equality, but superiority and payback. You will always be the bad guy.	I am unimportant. I am unworthy of being treated with respect.
Blank for Template	Romance 1st -Communicative, funny, unfaithful, addiction, lies, manipulation and abuse. 2nd – Loyal and kind. Surface Communication (some loneliness). Both find meaning in work.	Romance Bait & Switch – my issues 1st – Tolerated unacceptable behavior, desperate, and devalued 2nd – Ignore problems (lazy & easily frustrated), neglect relationship, work to avoid the emptiness.	Romance Men will pursue you until they get what they want, then you will be devalued. Men can take care of themselves, and don't need much attention.	Romance I am expendable, to be used up and thrown away. He is unimportant.

Template	Pattern	Eliciting Maneuver	Pathogenic Belief	Core Belief
Blank for Template	<u>Children</u> Anger – Irritable, isolating, Sad – Crying, isolating Spouse Anger – Sarcasm Spouse Sad – Void Joy – Spending time together, crafts, travel, special moments	<u>Adult Children</u> Very loving, but very distant. Anger & pain not discussed, don't want to hurt each other. Neglected relationship. Struggle with genuineness, but is very generous.	<u>Adult Children</u> <u>My child is very fragile physically and emotionally and cannot withstand confrontation. She will reject me or yell at me, if I discuss my feelings.</u>	<u>Adult Children</u> I am a failure. I am a bad mother. My child doesn't love me.

Chapter 6: Enhanced Learning Exercises Using the Relational Chart®

Once the chart is completed, use the following exercises to reinforce these concepts and applications.

1. Apply the Relational Chart® to a film. Years ago, I was blessed to come across a film that demonstrates this intervention beautifully. The film is called, "Nuts" (Ritt, 1987) staring Barbra Streisand. I recommend watching the film as a group and bringing a completed Relational Chart for Claudia Draper (Streisand's character) the following week. This exercise is often the group's first revelation of how much they have truly learned and can use this with clients.

2. Template Exercise. Have group members pair off and participate in a role-playing assessment/intake. Inform the group that they will have 15-20 minutes to gain as much information about client's template as possible. As a group, generate questions that are likely to produce this information. Some suggested questions are as follows: Where were you raised and by whom? How did you get along with your parents? What are your favorite memories of mom (dad, siblings, and/or family)? What are your least favorite memories with mom (dad, siblings, and/or family)? Discussions of symptoms and other mental status considerations will integrate naturally. Remember, that you won't have enough time at intake to build upon each item, so be sure to convey

empathy (especially with painful responses) and a desire to explore this further. Have each group member complete the template portion of the Relational Chart® based on the responses of their role-playing client. Discuss the exercise and methods of improving effectiveness and timeliness, while not losing the compassion and rapport building.

3. Pattern Exercise. For the purposes of congruence, have group members pair off with the same person they completed the Template Exercise with (if possible). Inform the group they will have 20-30 minutes to build upon the template portion of the assessment completed previously. As a group, generate questions that are likely to produce this information. Some suggested questions are as follows: What was school like academically and behaviorally? Who were your closest friends as a child, a teenager, and now as an adult? How did the childhood relationships end (if they did)? Tell me about your three most significant romantic relationships (strengths, weaknesses, length, and how they ended). Tell me about your employment (length, type, relationships with peers and supervisors and why each job ended). Discussions of symptoms and other mental status considerations will integrate naturally and should be welcomed. Remember, that you won't have enough time to build upon each item, so be sure to convey empathy (especially with painful responses) and a desire to explore this further. Have each group member complete the pattern portion of the Relational Chart®. Discuss the exercise and methods of improving effectiveness and timeliness, while not losing compassion and rapport building.

4. Complete the Eliciting Maneuvers Exercise. This is something the therapist initially does without the client by reviewing the client's responses to the template and pattern questions. Next, underline the similarities between the template and patterns and begin forming working hypotheses about their eliciting maneuvers.

For example, the client can't sustain employment, because all of their bosses are "idiots". In that case, it's fair to deduce (as a working hypotheses) that the client is evocative towards authority figures. *How might this surface in therapy?*

If each of the client's relationships have resulted in domestic violence, it's fair to deduce that your client may not recognize the early warning signs of domestic violence, may struggle to leave the relationship once violence occurs and has little belief in themselves. (Again, I'm not suggesting victim blaming, just identifying what behavior occurs that predicts reenactment.) *How might this surface in therapy?*

If your client is a top achiever with little or no friends, it may be the case that they assume control and resist collaboration. *How might this surface in therapy?*

If your client is constantly depressed about their romantic relationships, but never discusses this with their partner, that is also an eliciting maneuver. *How might this surface in therapy?*

Just one more thing... what does the client elicit in you? A desire to rescue, a desire to please, a desire to punish, a desire to reject or abandon (especially if they are evocative towards you), and/or a desire to refer? We could increase this list ad infinitum.

Next, look at the pattern list again. Does the client seem to elicit this response in other relationships as well? If the answer is "yes," you can use your experience to assist the client in recognizing their eliciting maneuvers and the undesired outcomes. If the answer is "no", it may be countertransference. Does this client remind you of someone in your past? Each group member should complete the eliciting maneuvers section of the Relational Chart®. This exercise tends to elicit some of the most beneficial group discussions. Examine how these eliciting maneuvers have or predictably may manifest in therapy. Role-play effective responses to eliciting maneuvers, such as, use of a process comments.

5.   Complete the Pathogenic Beliefs Exercise. There is a direct relationship between pathogenic beliefs and eliciting maneuvers. Review the template, pattern, and eliciting maneuvers section and ask yourself, "What beliefs keep this pattern repeating?" If the client was abandoned in youth and you note a pattern of abandonment, help the client to recognize what behaviors elicit abandonment and what *thoughts* trigger the behavior? It may be the case that the client believes that "all men leave anyway" and rather than deal with the anxiety of that cognition, they unconsciously elicit it. Think of pathogenic beliefs as closely related to Cognitive-Behavioral Therapy's (CBT) intermediate beliefs, rules or assumptions regarding relationships (Beck, 1995). You will also detect the client's pathogenic beliefs in their story telling and explanations for why things occur. Have your group again get into pairs for role-playing, preferably with the same partner from the previous exercises. Members will be given 15-20 minutes to review the Relational Chart® with the client. Ask your client if they recognize any patterns and maybe even eliciting maneuvers. Pause (5-10 minutes) the role play, and allow the therapist to examine this information and form working hypotheses about the client's pathogenic beliefs. Return to session for 5-10 minutes, and ask your client about their potential pathogenic beliefs (or test your hypotheses). For example, "I noticed that each of your romantic relationships lasts about 2 years. I'm wondering what your thoughts are about that (or relationship longevity in general)." "I noticed that you seem to put more effort into your relationships than your partners. Would you agree with that? If so, what do you think that's about?"

6.   Complete the Core Beliefs Exercise. It would be best to do this immediately following the pathogenic belief exercise, as you will generate your questions through the pathogenic beliefs. Take 5-10 minutes with the same partner from the pathogenic beliefs exercise to ask about their core beliefs. Remember that core beliefs operate under the "if / then" premise. "If (pathogenic belief) is true, then I

must be (core belief)." For example, if your relationships never last longer than two years, because "that's when they really get to know me," what does that say about you? You will often have to deal with a few more pathogenic beliefs before getting to the core belief. Think of it as an inverted triangle, where you may start broad and narrow and progress down to the tip or the core belief in this case.

For example:

Therapist: What do you tell yourself about always giving more than you get in relationships?

Client: Oh' you know, all men are lazy.

Therapist: All men are lazy?

Client: Well, not all of them, but the ones who date me. I'm no prize you know.

Therapist: What do you mean by "I'm no prize"?

Client: You know, I'm not pretty or skinny.

Therapist: So if only pretty and skinny women deserve a hard-working man, what does that say about how you see yourself? Client: I'm not worthy or deserving. (BINGO)

Chapter 7: Resistance

You may have a group member who cannot understand (or appreciate) these concepts, but it doesn't make it any less necessary to teach it. It would be impossible, as a student, to truly recognize the skills you are likely to need outside of the idealized academic environment, where clients do what they're told. You can't give someone something you don't have; if you do not understand your dynamics, this can be very intimidating. What if you're a therapist who has never worked through their own issues in a significant way? What if you've never "gone there" and more importantly, some of your instructors and employers have never experienced it and consequently, invalidate the importance of it? Who wouldn't rather approach things easily and inexpensively... but at what price to the clients and profession?

Our clients are suffering; We're losing them. It's about the client who finally comes to therapy in so much pain and having humbled themselves enough to ask for help is given a worksheet and deep breathing exercises. It's about the child client acting out because they were abused and the therapist providing them with a behavior chart. It's the client who has been binge-eating her molestation away and starts to weep and is redirected to use her WISEMIND (as cited in Tanning, 2019). While these interventions are wonderful at the right time and collaboration, it's easy to see why clients report feeling invalidated! Remember, therapy is not about you, the modality you were trained in, or what you feel comfortable with. It's about what the client's need and exercising enough depth to identify these needs.

Understanding the timing of interventions comes from understanding the client first. If you do not have relational skills, your therapy will not be collaborative, effective or meaningful. You will hurt people. There are few things worse than feeling invalidated by the world, only to be invalidated by your therapist too! Learning these skills is an investment into the profession, and your ego (fear) should never usurp the needs of the client.

Chapter 8: Coping with Your New Role

"I feel like John Coffey from the movie The Green Mile (Darabont, 1999). People open their mouths, and I take in all of their pain."

– Intern (2010)

"I've come to believe that some clients are like vampires. They latch onto your neck and suck you dry... then move onto someone else."

– Veteran Therapist (2018)

Since this book is addressed primarily to new therapists, one more concept should be a centerpiece in your program, but likely has been given only superficial attention. These are the concepts of self-care and burn-out. You are a new therapist who likely has always listened to and helped solve people's problems and found it deeply gratifying, but now you're doing it eight hours a day. Like the notion of the shoemaker's kids having no shoes, the last thing you want to do when you get home is listen to anyone's problems. You may sit (in a coma-like state) in front of the television, while a small bit of drool collects on the side of your mouth. You are realizing that a lot of people you once called friends are really unpaid clients with your personal phone number. There are times when only love and obligation pushes you to continue to provide for those closest to you...because you're exhausted.

As an intern (associate), you are likely working at a governmental or non-profit agency that is short-staffed with an abundance of needy clients. You entered the profession because you genuinely wanted to help people, but the line of clients is never ending. You notice that some of your colleagues, especially those who have been practicing for a long time, do not seem eager to help these clients. In fact, they seem cynical about the clients and the possibility of change, which appears to justify (in their minds) the denial of services. Simply stated, they are burnt out... but they didn't start out that way. They have been giving and giving for years with little replenishment. They may feel stuck, as they owe thousands of dollars in student loans, and/or need a stable profession and income.

When a therapist reaches this place, they may purchase a book or go to a workshop designed to prevent burn-out. The therapist is told that self-care is the answer. That is to suggest that if you're burn-out, it's the result of poor self-care (or your fault). This is a lie.

Listening to people's pain for eight hours a day is unnatural, and burnout is a logical consequence.

The burnt-out therapist is a normal reaction to an abnormal situation. It is unlikely that anyone can be fed enough to continue to feed others at this pace. If you're a loving and effective therapist, you will become burnt-out at some point, because good therapy demands significant cognitive and emotional energy. No amount of yoga will change this. Contrary to being ashamed of burn-out, consider that you could be a therapist who has given so little of yourself that you're just fine... but I bet your clients aren't.

Let's approach burn-out as something not to be avoided, but something that is inevitable and not to be dealt with through denial, but with a solid plan. As a therapist, you have entered a profession with many outlets and possibilities, especially if you work for a governmental agency. For example, the psychological demands of working a crisis intervention unit are different than the demands of conducting traditional therapy. The crisis unit requires you to be calm, act quickly and put out the proverbial fires. There's something different every day. Traditional therapy demands thinking beyond the crisis and exploring long-term solutions. It can be deeply gratifying, but also monotonous and grueling. As therapists, we can be hired in many capacities like the following: doing intakes at the county jail, facilitating brief court-ordered programs, working in the field, working at the hospital, working residential treatment, teaching, etc. ***To avoid burn-out, be prepared to change roles***. If you're exhausted from conducting traditional therapy, put out fires for a while. If you're seeking greater meaning in therapy, look at traditional work. Whenever possible, accept employment at an agency that has many different programs, so you can transfer without losing benefits, pension…or belief in yourself.

You may need to change your playground and playmates. As previously stated, therapists' relationships are often emotionally laden. To quote my daughter (in elementary school), ***"Your work cannot be your extra-curricular activity."*** Let that sink in! When you are not at work, you will need to find friends in the classic definition, or a bidirectional relationship (not a unidirectional relationship like in therapy). You may not currently have many bidirectional relationships, as many therapists are accustomed to playing therapist with everyone. While it's exhausting, it also provides you with a degree of control and ensures not having to be vulnerable (secondary gain). You are the teacher; they are the student. You are the doctor; they are the patient. Some therapists have never experienced a relationship, where they truly walked shoulder-to-shoulder with someone - not in front of them, not behind them, but beside them. It is the nature of some therapists to always walk ahead. Who are you, if you're not the person who provides the answers to family and friends?

It's a little scary, but the true friendships that await you will be profoundly more gratifying. You may even find that pathogenic and core beliefs made you believe that your worth and value were in what you could supply to others. You may need to learn vulnerability. Your friend is your equal, not your patient to treat. In friendship, there will be times when you will support your friends and times when they will support you, but mostly you will share common interests and have fun! What a concept! What do you enjoy doing, when you're not saving the world?

I deeply honor your commitment to becoming a therapist. Thank you for the services that you will provide. You have a generous heart and a compassionate spirit. You will need to take care of yourself, but that's defined differently for each person. Remember, we cannot heal our wounds vicariously and the more unresolved issues we have, the more likely we are to hurt others unconsciously.

This is a profession like no other. You can build houses and work with computers, and you won't have to care about your relational dynamics or anyone else's. Even if you teach or entertain, the depth of understanding is less. My conclusions come from 25 years of doing therapy, 20 years of teaching and supervising therapists, reading well over 200 client complaints about therapists, and observing an overall gradual and unintentional decline in the quality of care. I beset you to care enough about our clients, yourself and what's at stake to be courageous and continue self-exploration and growth. This is a beginning, not an end.

Appendix A: Finding Your Template

Finding Your Template®

1. What city and state did you grow up in?

2. As a child, did you feel safe in your neighborhood?

3. Were there other children to play with in your neighborhood?

4. Did you play with other children in the neighborhood independent of direct parental supervision?

5. How often did your family move? If you moved more than once, what was the reason for the moves?

6. Describe your experiences (if any) with the church, as a child.

7. What concept (if any) of God did you have as a child?

8. How would you describe your parents' financial situation? (circle one)
   A. Impoverished - Unemployed or underemployed didn't always have money for the basics
   B. Working class - Income from employment, always met basic needs, but extras were rare
   C. Middle class - Income from employment, safe suburbs, ability to meet basic needs and many extras (like sports, band, etc.), College, and some domestic travel
   D. Upper middle class - A minimum of twice the average income for one's state (but less than the working wealthy) through employment, upscale neighborhoods, some private schooling, college, domestic and some world travel.
   E. Nuevo Riche - Income comparable with the working wealthy or wealthy, but "new money" – so the education, social standing and power of the working wealthy and wealthy do not apply to this group, like most musicians and athletes.
   F. Working wealthy - Generational transmission of wealth through employment - family owned/operated corporations, like Sam Walton of Walmart.
   G. Wealthy – Old money, the *multigenerational transmission of wealth through inheritance*, political influence, and significant influence over domestic and world issues.

9. What was the marital status of your parents?

10. How did your parents handle anger towards each other? If applicable, describe two arguments you overheard as a child.

11. How did you (as a child) know that your mom was angry? What would she do?

12. How did you (as a child) know that your father was angry? What would he do?

13. How did you (as a child) know that your mom was sad? What would she do?

14. How did you (as a child) know that your dad was sad? What would he do?

15. What are your favorite memories **(at least three)** of your mother?

16. What are your favorite memories **(at least three)** of your father?

17. Did your father work (outside of the home) consistently? If yes, what did outside employment mean to him? What were his household duties?

18. Did your mother work (outside of the home) with consistency? If yes, what did outside employment mean to her? What were her household duties?

19. What are your earliest memories of childhood?

20. What is your birth order?

21. If applicable, describe your sibling(s).

22. How did you get along with your sibling(s)?

23. Did you ever feel like you and your siblings were competing? If so, describe.

24. As a child or teenager, describe a time you felt betrayed by a sibling(s).

25. As a child or teenager, describe a time you felt supported by a sibling(s).

26. Has a parent ever gossiped about a sibling to you? Vice-Versa.

27. Did a parent give you (or a sibling) authority over the other children?

28. What was your role in the family (hero, scapegoat, class clown, lost child)? Circle One.

    Hero – Excelled as a student or athlete or special talent. The family's pride and joy.

    Scapegoat – The child that was always in trouble. The "problem" child.

    Class Clown – The entertaining child that helped the rest of the family to deflect.

    Lost Child – Isolating. Little or no voice within the family. Stopped seeking attention

29. Describe **two** conflicts you had with the parent of the same gender.

30. Did you ever sense that the parent of the same gender was jealous of you and/or engaged in a power struggle with you?

31. Describe times that you felt betrayed by the parent of the same gender.

32. Describe times you felt supported by the parent of the same gender.

33. Did you feel like the parent of the opposite gender respected the parent of the same gender?

34. Describe **two** conflicts you had with the parent of the opposite gender.

35. Did you ever sense that the parent of the opposite gender was jealous of you and engaged in a power struggle with you?

36. Describe times that you felt betrayed by the parent of the opposite gender.

37. Describe times you felt supported by the parents of the opposite gender.

38. Was there ever a time that you were asked by one parent to keep a secret from the other? Describe.

39. How would you describe your ethnicity?

40. Was your family apart of any subculture like the following: military, gangs, LGBTQ, strict or unconventional religion, welfare (poverty), etc.

41. What did your mother tell you to expect from society based on your ethnicity?

42. What did your father tell you to expect from society based on your ethnicity?

43. If applicable, describe at least two incidences of discrimination from your childhood.

Appendix B: Finding Your Patterns

Finding Your Patterns®

1. To the best of your recollection, describe your friendships in elementary school. Did you have many friends or just a few? Longterm?

2. Describe two positive experiences with friends in elementary school.

3. Describe two negative experiences with friends in elementary school.

4. Describe two positive experiences with teachers in elementary school.

5. Describe two negative experiences with teachers in elementary school.

6. Describe your friendships in middle school. Did you have many friends or just a few? Long-term friendships?

7. Describe two positive experiences with friends in middle school.

8. Describe two negative experiences with friends in middle school.

9. Describe two positive experiences with teachers in middle school.

10. Describe two negative experiences with teachers in middle school.

11. Describe your friendships in high school. Did you have many friends or just a few? Long-term friendships?

12. Describe two positive experiences with friends in high school.

13. Describe two negative experiences with friends in high school.

14. Describe two positive experiences with teachers in high school.

15. Describe two negative experiences with a teacher in high school.

16. Who was your first serious boyfriend or girlfriend? How old were you?

17. Describe your first serious romantic relationship. How long did it last? How were conflicts handled in the relationship? How did it end?

18. Describe your second serious romantic relationship. How long did it last? How were conflicts handled in the relationship? How did it end?

19. Describe your third serious romantic relationship. How long did it last? How were conflicts handled in the relationship? How did it end?

20. Describe any other serious romantic relationships (except the current one)? How long did they last? How were conflicts handled in those relationships? How did they end?

Current Status

21. What city / state have you resided in for most of your adult life?

22. Have you felt safe in your neighborhood for most of your adult life?

23. Describe your interactions (if any) with your neighbors.

24. If applicable, are there children in your neighborhood who frequently interact with your children?

25. If your children are 10 or older, can they enjoy a degree of freedom (e.g., no direct supervision) when interacting with friends?

26. In your adult life, how many times have you moved? If more than once, what was the reason for these moves?

27. Do you have a religious / spiritual preference? Do you attend church at least once a week?

28. What is your concept of God?

29. How would you describe your (and your spouse if applicable) financial situation? (circle one)

    A. Impoverished - Unemployed or underemployed and don't always have money for the basics
    B. Working class - Income from employment, always meet basic needs, but extras are rare
    C. Middle class - Income from employment, safe suburbs, ability to meet basic needs and many extras (like sports, band, etc.), College, and some domestic travel

    D. Upper middle class - At minimum of twice the average income for one's state (but less than the working wealthy) through employment, upscale neighborhoods, some private schooling, college, domestic and some world travel.

    E. Nuevo Riche - Income comparable with the working wealthy or wealthy, but "new money" – so the education, social standing and power of the working wealthy and wealthy do not apply to this group, often musicians and athletes belong to this group.

    F. Working wealthy - Generational transmission of wealth through employment - family owned / operated corporations, like Sam Walton of Walmart.

    G. Wealthy – Old money, the *multigenerational transmission of wealth through inheritance*, political influence, and significant influence over domestic and world issues.

30. What is your marital status? Any divorces, separations, etc. If you are single (not married or in a long-term cohabitating relationship), skip to item 33. If you are single (not married or in a longterm cohabitating relationship) AND childless, skip to item 40.

31. How do you handle conflicts with your spouse? Describe a recent conflict.

32. What are your favorite memories **(at least three)** of interactions with your spouse?

33. How do your children know you're angry (e.g., behaviors, words, etc.)?

34. How do your children know your spouse is angry (e.g., behaviors, words, etc.)?

35. How do your children know when you're sad (e.g., behaviors, words, etc.)?

36. How do your children know when your spouse is sad (e.g., behaviors, words, etc.)?

37. What are your favorite memories **(at least three)** of interactions with your children?

38. What are your favorite memories **(at least three)** of your children's interactions with your spouse?

39. What are your favorite memories **(at least three)** of interactions with the entire family?

40. Describe your work life. What does work mean to you? In an average week, how much time do you spend at work?

41. Describe your spouse's work life. What does work mean them? In an average week, how much time does your spouse spend at work?

42. What is the division of labor (household duties) between you and your spouse? How do you feel about this division?

43. If applicable, what is the division of childcare duties between you and your spouse? How do you feel about this division?

44. While parents typically love ALL of their children, which child do you identify with the most, and why? What is their birth order?

45. Describe your friends and colleagues now. Many friends? Few close friends?

46. How well do you get along with friends and colleagues?

47. How long do your friendships typically last?

48. Do you ever feel like you and your friends or colleagues are competing? If so, describe.

49. Describe a time that you felt betrayed by a friend or colleague.

50. Describe a time that you felt supported by a friend or colleague.

51. Have you ever attempted to undermine a supervisor's authority? (Think hard. If you've gone over their head (even if you felt it was justified), you have done this. If you have negatively gossiped with coworkers about your supervisor, you have done this.)

52. Without a promotion or change of title, has a supervisor ever given you (or a colleague) authority over peers? Do you have a special de facto role at work, like the birthday person, the donut bringer, the crisis counselor, etc.

53. What is your role at work (e.g., hero, scapegoat, class clown, lost child, etc.)? (Circle one)

    Hero – Great performer. The person others go to for problem-solving. The fix-it person. Scapegoat – The employee who underperforms. The "problem child" of the office.

    Class Clown – The entertaining employee (jokes, and pranks) especially when the office is stressed. Lost Child – Isolating. Little or no voice at work. They never cause problems, but also never stands out.

    Scapegoat – Tends to get blamed for problems at work.

    Lost Child – Keep to yourself. Few Peers.

54. Did you ever sense that a supervisor was threatened by you and engaged in a power struggle?

55. Do you respect for your supervisor, or are you sure you could do it better?

56. Was there ever a time you were in a position to align with one supervisor against another? Describe.

57. Describe times that you felt betrayed by a supervisor.

58. Describe times that you felt supported by a supervisor.

59. As an adult, how would you describe your ethnicity.

60. Is your family part of a subculture like the following: military, gangs, LGBTQ, a strict or unconventional religion, welfare (poverty), etc.

61. If applicable, describe instances of discrimination based on your culture or subculture.

62. What do you (or your spouse) tell your children to expect from society, based on your ethnicity or subculture membership?

Appendix C: Finding Your Eliciting Maneuvers

Finding Your Eliciting Maneuvers®

1. How did you prepare to support yourself (e.g., college, work, military, etc.)?

2. How did you choose the neighborhood you currently reside in?

3. Did you rent or buy your residence?

4. Do you attend church (or other spiritual programs) weekly? In a given week, how much time do you spend engaged in reading, praying, meditating, church, etc.?

5. What do my relationships with female authority figures and my relationship with my mother have in common? (Go to your Relational Chart and look at templates and patterns thus far.)

6. What do my relationships with male authority figures and my relationship with my mother have in common?

7. What is my initial reaction when I meet a female authority figure? What thoughts do I have?

8. How do I contribute to continued positive or negative exchanges with female authority figures? (Close your eyes and imagine that you are the boss. How might you react to someone like you?)

9. What types of behaviors are "red flags" that a relationship with a female authority figure is not safe?

10. Describe how feeling threatened impacts your actions or attitudes.

11. Can you think of a time when your assumptions about a female authority figure were wrong?

12. If I feel betrayed by a female authority figure, I react by _____.

13. Could changing your reaction and thinking, impact the relationship? (If yes, how so? If not, think again.)

14. What do my relationships with female authority figures and my relationship with my father have in common?

15. What do my relationships with male authority figures and my relationship with my father have in common?

16. What is my initial reaction when I meet a male authority figure? What are my thoughts?

17. How do I contribute to continued positive or negative exchanges with male authority figures? (Close your eyes and imagine that you are the boss. How might you react to someone like you?)

18. Could my initial reactions be evoking the male authority figures responses? If yes, how so? (If not, think again.)

19. What types of behaviors are "red flags" that a relationship with a male authority figure is not safe?

20. Describe how feeling threatened impacts your actions or attitudes.

21. Can you think of a time when your assumptions about a male authority figure were wrong?

22. If I feel betrayed by a male authority figures, I react by _____.

23. Could changing your reaction and thinking, impact the relationship? (If yes, how so? If not, think again.)

24. What do my relationships with peers (friends and colleagues) and my relationship with my siblings have in common?

25. What is my initial reaction when I meet a new peer? What are my thoughts?

26. Could my initial reactions be evoking the peer's response? If yes, how so? (If not, think again.)

27. How do I contribute to continued positive or negative exchanges with peers? (Close your eyes and imagine that you are one of your peers. How might you react to someone like you?)

28. If I feel betrayed by a peer, I react by _____.

29. What types of behaviors are "red flags" that a relationship with a peer is not safe?

30. Describe how feeling threatened impacts your actions or attitudes.

31. Can you think of a time when your assumptions about a peer were wrong?

32. Could changing your reaction / thinking, impact the relationship? (If yes, how so? If not, think again.)

33. What do my relationships with romantic partners have in common with my parents' relationship?

34. Historically, how do I respond when I meet someone I am romantically interested in? Does my personality change? Describe your "best self" or what you present in the first year of a relationship?

35. How does your presentation in romantic relationships change with time? Describe your "comfortable self".

36. What types of behaviors are "red flags" that a partner is not safe (interpersonally or otherwise)?

37. Describe how feeling threatened impacts your actions or attitudes towards your partner.

38. Can you think of a time when your assumptions about a partner were wrong?

39. What are the things my partner says and does that I find most painful?

40. What is my reaction to my partner's above behavior? What do I tell myself about my partner's motive for their behavior?

41. If my reaction to the behavior (or thoughts) changed, would my partner's response be different? (If yes, how so. If not, think again.)

42. How much time to you spend alone with your partner in a given week? How much of this time is spent talking?

43. When was the last time you did something you didn't want to do, because your partner wanted it?

44. In a given month, how much time do you spend reflecting on your relationship with your partner?

45. How are my relationships with my children similar to my mother's relationship with me?
    What behavior of mine is similar to my mother's?

46. How are my relationships with my children similar to my father's relationship with me? What behavior of mine is similar to my father's?

47. How many waking hours do you spend with your children in a given day?

48. How much of that time is spent (exclusively) engaged in talking and / or non-media related activities?

49. In a given month, how much time do you ponder ways to improve your relationship with your children?

50. Describe the attitudes or behaviors that have brought you the most pain from your children.

51. What do you tell yourself about the above behavior?

52. Could my initial reactions be evoking the responses? If yes, how so? (If not, think again.)

53. How do I contribute to continued positive or negative exchanges with my children? (Close your eyes and imagine that you are your child. How might you react to someone like you?)

54. What types of behaviors are "red flags" that I might have a negative exchange with my child(ren)?

55. Describe how feeling threatened impacts your actions or attitudes with your children.

56. Can you think of a time when your assumptions about your child(ren) were wrong?

57. If I feel betrayed by my child(ren), I react by _____.

58. Could changing your reaction / thinking, impact the relationship? (If yes, how so? If not, think again.)

59. How would you describe your ethnicity? Include subculture groups like LGBTQ membership, religious / church membership, economic class, military, gangs, etc.)

60. Do you confront people if you think they are being racist, homophobic, etc.? Why or why not?

61. Have your ever attributed someone's attitude and behavior to racism (homophobia, etc.) and later discovered that the attitude and behavior was due to something else?

62. Do you assume when you are rejected (disliked) that it's due to your ethnicity and/or membership in a subculture?

63. Is part of my ethnicity or subculture membership involved in focusing on how my group has been wronged and by whom?

64. Do you believe that your ethnic group and / or subculture are superior to some other ethnicities and subcultures? Why or why not?

65. Do the people you interact with most (especially family) tend to tell racial (sexual orientation, etc.) jokes and suggest demeaning things about other groups? Would you be embarrassed if a friend of another ethnicity heard your family or friends speak this way? Do you justify or minimize their behavior?

66. Do you notice behaviors of other ethnicities and groups that do NOT fit stereotypes?

67. Outside of work, do you have a **close** friend of another ethnicity?

68. Is your ethnicity or subculture membership a significant portion of your identity? That is, do you spend significant time with members of your group and/or advocating for your group's causes?

69. Could changing your reaction and thinking, impact your relationships with those outside of your ethnicity and/or subculture? (If yes, how so? If not, think again.)

Appendix D: Finding Your Pathogenic Beliefs

Finding Your Pathogenic Beliefs®

(Use your Relational Chart)

1. **Look at your demographic eliciting maneuvers. What beliefs drive your demographic choices?** For example, your demographic eliciting maneuvers suggest that you work 80 hours a week (despite health issues) to ensure that your family can live in an affluent neighborhood. The pathogenic beliefs that drive this behavior could be as follows: Money is more important than my health. Good fathers (mothers) ensure that their families live in affluent neighborhoods. If I didn't provide this, my family wouldn't love me and my spouse might leave.

2. **Look at your female authority eliciting maneuvers. What do you tell yourself about a person or situation that causes you to act according to your eliciting maneuvers?** For example, you are automatically suspicious of female authority figures. Your pathogenic belief could be that women can't be trusted.

3. **Look at your male authority eliciting maneuvers. What do you tell yourself about a person or situation that causes you to act according to your eliciting maneuvers?** For example, you dismiss it when your boss assigns most of his work to you. Your pathogenic beliefs could be that he wouldn't give me extra work if he weren't really busy (even if you know that's not true).

   Look at your peer eliciting maneuvers. What do you tell yourself about a person or situation that causes you to act according to your eliciting maneuvers? For example, you spend a minimal amount of time pursuing friendships. Your pathogenic beliefs could be that people are users and therefore, friendships are not worth pursuing.

4. **Look at your God / Religion (under culture) eliciting maneuvers. What do you tell yourself about God or religion that causes you to act according to your eliciting maneuvers?** For example, you only turn to God in a crisis and don't attend church. Your pathogenic beliefs could be, I only need God in a crisis, and church people are hypocrites.

5. **Look at your cultural eliciting maneuvers. What do you tell yourself about a person or situation that causes you to act according to your eliciting maneuvers?** For example, I get angry when I see my ethnicity being mocked. My pathogenic belief could be that mocking my ethnicity is culturally sanctioned.

Look at your romantic relationship eliciting maneuvers. What do you tell yourself about a person or situation that causes you to act according to your eliciting maneuvers? For example, you have stayed in a relationship with an unfaithful partner. Your pathogenic beliefs could be that all men (women) are unfaithful, or he (she) is unfaithful because I've gained weight.

6. **Look at your child(ren) eliciting maneuvers. What do you tell yourself about a person or situation that causes you to act according to your eliciting maneuvers?** For example, you don't call your adult children. Your pathogenic beliefs could be that they would call if they loved me, or they don't want to talk to me.

7. **Look at the themes of your eliciting maneuvers. What do you tell yourself about a person or situation that causes you to act according to your eliciting maneuvers?** For example, all of my eliciting maneuvers suggest that I don't invest much into relationships, because "people take and take and then they leave you." My pathogenic beliefs are that people are users and not worth the investment. When the money (efforts) are gone, so it the love.

Appendix E: Finding Your Core Beliefs

Finding Your Core Beliefs®

(Use Your Relational Chart)

Core beliefs are what we have decided about ourselves (once we strip away the defense mechanisms), based on our relationship patterns. The core belief can be found by questioning your pathogenic beliefs, BUT this is often task best done with a trusted other. Our initial responses are not generally our core beliefs, but other pathogenic beliefs. Finding core beliefs takes a bit of digging. Some of you will be able to do this for yourself, but there's no shame in asking a trusted person to help you narrow your beliefs. For example:

Therapist: So, you believe that all men will hurt you (pathogenic belief)? If all men will hurt you, what about **you** that makes this true? They don't hurt everyone. Why you?

Client: I guess because I put up with so much crap.

Therapist: …but why do you put up with so much crap? Why you? You said your friend Emily doesn't take any crap. What about you that makes it okay for others to give you so much crap?

Client: I just don't want to be alone.

Therapist: So, you have put up with crap to not be alone? How come Emily doesn't put up with crap to not be alone?

Client: Well, she's beautiful.

Therapist: Do you have to be beautiful to be treated with respect?

Client: Look, he's the best I can do.

Therapist: Why? Why is he the best you can do? What about you only makes you worthy of someone who treats you like crap?

Client: I'm nothing okay! My own father didn't want me. I'm fat and ugly… I'm nothing! I should be grateful that somebody is there.

The core belief, in this case is, "I am nothing." Notice that it took a bit of time to get there. Core beliefs touch upon our shame, and it is natural to do everything possible to avoid shame. Unfortunately, shame exists whether or not we speak to it, and revealing it is key to healing it!

1. **Look at your demographic pathogenic beliefs. Use an "if / then" formula, or "If (pathogenic belief) is true, then what does it say about me?' (Core belief).** For example, "If money is more important than my health, then I must not be very important." "If my wife will leave me if I don't make good money, then I must be unimportant and unloved."

2. **Look at your female authority figure pathogenic beliefs. Use an "if / then" formula, or "If (pathogenic belief) is true, then what does it say about me?" (Core belief).** For example, "If all women are out to get me, then I must be unworthy of a woman's love and protection."

3. **Look at your male authority pathogenic beliefs. Use an "if / then" formula, or "If (pathogenic belief) is true, then what does it say about me?" (Core belief).** For example, "If my boss assigns me most of his work and not others, then my time (me) must not be very important."

4. **Look at your peer pathogenic beliefs. Use an "if/then" formula, or "If (pathogenic belief) is true, then what does it say about me?" (Core belief).** For example, "If my friends leave when the money is gone, then I'm not lovable myself."

5. **Look at your romantic relationship pathogenic beliefs. Use an "if / then" formula, or "If (pathogenic belief) is true, then what does it say about me? (Core belief).** For example, "If gaining weight makes me unattractive and undeserving of my partner's fidelity, then I must be unlovable."

6. **Look at your pathogenic beliefs about your children. Use an "if / then" formula, or "If (pathogenic belief) is true, then what does it say about me? (Core belief).** For example, "If children who love their parents call them (and my children don't call), then I must be unloved."

7. **Look at your pathogenic beliefs about your culture (including God and religion, if applicable). Use an "if / then" formula, or "If (pathogenic belief) is true, then what does it say about me?" (Core belief).** For example, if curvy bodies are sexy (and I don't have one), then I'm inferior.

Appendix F: Relational Chart Key

Relational Chart Key®

Template Worksheet

Directions: On your chart create the following categories in the Template section: demographics, mother, father, siblings, and culture. Place your responses to the worksheet questions in the category indicated below. Demographics: 1, 2, 3, 4, 5, 6, 7, 8, 9, 20, 28

Mother: 10, 11, 13, 15, 18, 19. (29 – 33, and 38 for women, 29, and 33-38 for men)

Father: 10, 12, 14, 16, 17, 19. (33-38 for women, 29-33 and 38 for men)

Siblings: 21-27

Culture: 38-43

Patterns Worksheet

Directions: On your chart create the following categories in the Patterns section: demographics, female authority, male authority, romance, children, friends/coworkers, and culture. Some numbers are in two categories, because the authority figure could have been male or female. Place your responses to the worksheet questions in the category indicated below.

Demographics: 21-26, 29, 30 and 53

Female authority: 4, 5, 9, 10, 14, 15, 51, 52, 54, 55, 56, 57, and 58

Male authority: 4, 5, 9, 10, 14, 15, 51, 52, 54, 55, 56, 57, and 58

Romance: 16-20, 31 and 32

Children: 33-44

Friends / Colleagues: 1-3, 6-8, 11-13, and 45-50

Culture: 59-62

Eliciting Maneuvers Worksheet

Directions: On your chart create the following categories in the Eliciting Maneuvers section: demographics, female authority, male authority, romance, children, friends/coworkers, children and culture. Place your responses to the worksheet questions in the category indicated below.

Appendix F: Relational Chart Key

Demographics: 1, 2, 3,

Female Authority: 5-14,

Male Authority: 15-23

Romance: 34-45

Children: 46-59

Friends / Colleagues: 24-32

Culture: 4 and 59-69

Pathogenic Beliefs Worksheet

Directions: On your large chart create the following categories in the Pathogenic Beliefs section: demographics, female authority, male authority, romance, children, friends/coworkers, children and culture. Place your responses to the worksheet questions in the category indicated below.

Demographics: 1

Female Authority: 2

Male Authority: 3

Friend / Colleague: 4

Romance: 7

Children: 8

Culture: 5 and 6

Core Beliefs Worksheet

Directions: On your chart create the following categories in the Core Beliefs section: demographics, female authority, male authority, romance, children, friends/coworkers, children and culture. Place your responses to the worksheet questions in the category indicated below.

Demographics: 1

Female Authority: 2

Male Authority: 3

Friend / Colleague: 4

Romance: 5

Children: 6

Culture: 6

Appendix G: Blank Relational Chart®

Template	Pattern	Eliciting Maneuver	Pathogenic Belief	Core Belief

Glossary

Corrective Emotional Experience – "1. An experience through which one comes to understand an event or relationship in a different or unexpected way that results in an emotional coming to terms with it. 2. Originally, a concept from psychoanalysis positing that clients achieve meaningful and lasting change through new interpersonal affective experiences with the therapist, particularly with regard to situations that the clients were unable to master as children, (originally described in 1946 by Hungarian psychoanalyst Franz Alexander (1891-1964) and U.S. physician Thomas Morton French (b. 1892)" (APA, 2022). When the therapist does not respond to the client's eliciting maneuvers in a predictable way. For example, if a client responds to anxiety or shame by becoming antagonistic, the therapist doesn't respond to the antagonism with same rejection and/or avoidance of the topic or person that others do. Instead, a therapist will likely make a process comment and explore the defense mechanism.

Eliciting Maneuver – "An interpersonal strategy that wards off anxiety and brings about certain desired, safe responses" (Teyber, as cited on https://quizlet.com/169622658/teyber-teyber-chapter-8-flash-cards/).
How we get people to behave in a predictable way, or meet our relational expectations. For example, if someone is constantly being abandoned, it may be their behavior (i.e., infidelity, antagonism, passivity, etc.) that triggers others to abandon them.

Empathic Failure – "1. A lack of understanding of another person's feelings, perceptions, and thoughts. In self-psychology, a parent or caregiver's repeated empathic failure toward a child is thought to be a potential source of later psychopathology, such as narcissistic personality disorder and borderline personality disorder. 2. In psychoanalysis, a situation in which a patient feels misunderstood by the therapist or analyst. Compare attunement; misattunement. (first described in 1966 by Austrian-Born U.S. psychoanalyst Heinz Kohut (1913-1981)" (APA.2022). When the client feels misunderstood, judged, or invalidated by the therapist.

Internal Working Model of Attachment – "A cognitive construction or set of assumptions about the workings of relationships, such as expectations of support or affection. The earliest relationships may form the template for this internal model, which may be positive or negative. See also attachment theory (originally proposed by John Bowlby)" (APA, 2022). The relational templates that are reenacted based on conscious and unconscious eliciting maneuvers, pathogenic beliefs, and core beliefs.

References

American Psychological Association. (2022). Corrective emotional Experience. APA Dictionary of Psychology. . https://dictionary.apa.org/corrective-emotional-experience

American Psychological Association. (2022). Empathic failure. *APA Dictionary of Psychology.* https://dictionary.apa.org/empathic-failure

American Psychological Association. (2022). Internal working model of attachment. *APA Dictionary of Psychology.* *https://dictionary.apa.org/internal-working-model-of-attachment*

Ardito, R., Rabellino, D. (2011). Therapeutic alliance and outcome of psychotherapy: Historical excursus, measurements, prospects for research. *Frontiers in Psychology, 2(270).* *https://www.frontiersin.org/articles/10.3389/fpsyg.2011.00270/full*

Beck, Judith. (1995). *Cognitive therapy: Basics and beyond.* Guilford Publication.

Bowlby, J. (1958). The nature of the child's tie to his mother. *International Journal of Psycho-Analysis, 39*, 350-375. https://www.psychology.sunysb. edu.

California Health Care Foundation. (2018). *Mental health almanac: For too many, care not there.* https://www.chcf.org/wp-content/uploads/2018/03/ MentalHealthCalifornia2018.pdf

DeAngelis, T. (2019). Better relationships with patients lead to better outcomes, *American Psychological Association, 50(10).* https://www.APA.org Darabont, F. (1999). *The green mile* (Film). Castle Rock Entertainment & Darkwoods Productions.

Hutchings, K. (2022). "We have never seen such an egregious case': Inside Kaiser's broken mental health care system. *Fast Company.* https://www. fastcompany.com/90631941/we-have-never-seen-such-an-egregiouscase-inside-kaisers-broken-mental-health-care-system

Knobloch-Fedders, L. (2022)/ The importance of the relationships with the therapist. *Clinical Science Insights, 1,* https://www.family-institute.org/sites/default/files/pdfs/csi_fedders_relationship_with_therapist.pdf

Li, P. (2022). What is the internal working model of attachment. *Parenting for the Brain,* https://www.parentingforbrain.com/internal-working-model/

Miller, G. (2021). What is corrective emotional experience? *PsychCentral.*https://psychcentral.com/lib/what-is-corrective-Emotional experience#:~:text=What%20is%20a%20corrective%20emotionalshaped%20 your%20reactions%20and%20behaviors.

Miller, K. (2022). 7 solution-focused therapy techniques and worksheets. *Positive Psychology.* https://positivepsychology.com/solution-focused-therapy-techniques-worksheets/

Moore, C. (2019). Acceptance & commitment therapy: 21ACT worksheets. *Positive Psychology.* https://positivepsychology.com/act-worksheets/ O'Rear, C. (2014). Psychotherapy: Empathic failures, great & small. *LinkedIn.* https://www.linkedin.com/pulse/20141112142434-35949249-psychotherapy-empathic-failures-great-small

Ritt, M. (1997). *Nuts* (Film). Barwood Films.

Simran. (2022). Object relations: Meaning, uses, techniques, goals, benefits and limitations. *TherapyMantra.* https://therapymantra.co/therapy-types/ object-relations/

Stargell, N. (2017). Therapeutic relationship and outcome effectiveness: Implications for counselor educators. *The Journal of Counselor Preparation and Supervision, 9(2).* https://scholar.google.com/scholar_url?url=https://digitalcommons.sacredheart.edu/cgi/viewcontent.cgi%3Farticle%3D1164%26context%3Djcps&hl=en&sa=X&ei=u4hyY766OrOO6rQPsvut6Ao&scisig=AAGBfm1Xn0Jali8f-YkqbuDR3PM_fO15_w&oi=scholarr

Tanning, D. & A. (2019). Wise mind of mindfulness. https://r.search.yahoo.com/_ylt=AwrUixOBlHJjrD0A6gYPxQt.;_ylu=Y29sbwNncTEEcG9zAzUEdnRpZAMEc2VjA3Ny/RV=2/RE=1668482306/RO=10/RU=https%3a%2f%2fpeerguideddbtlessons.weebly.com%2fuploads%2f8_%2f2%2f0%2f9%2f82096548%2f1-5_mindfulness_wise_mind.pdf/RK=2/RS=XTRGMGNWVVmme9duoO3xIC_uXY8-

Teyber, E. (2000). *Interpersonal process in psychotherapy: A relational approach.* Brooks Cole.

Teyber & Teyber. (2022). *Eliciting Maneuver.* https://quizlet.com/169622658/teyber-teyber-chapter-8-flash-cards/

United States Copyright Office. (2014). *Relational Chart.* TX 8-018-427.

www.ingramcontent.com/pod-product-compliance
Lightning Source LLC
Chambersburg PA
CBHW070248290326
41930CB00042B/2932